The
Great American

DOG
Dr. Alvin Grossman

SHOW

GAME

Illustrated by Joseph Murray

Edited by
William W. Denlinger and R. Annabel Rathman

DENLINGER'S PUBLISHERS, LTD.
Box 76, Fairfax, Virginia 22030

Dedication

To my wives, Marjorie and Doris. Seldom has a man been so doubly blessed.

Library of Congress Cataloging in Publication Data

Grossman, Alvin.
    The great American dog show game.

    1. Dog shows—United States.   I. Denlinger,
William Watson.   II. Rathman, R. Annabel.
III. Title.
SF425.15.G76   1985   636.7'0888   83-24061
ISBN 0-87714-109-6

International Standard Book Number: 0-87714-109-6

Foreword

I have long felt that the lack of a good, informational program has severely hindered the "dog game." Newcomers gain information on a hit-or-miss basis, with no one attempting to provide for their overall guidance.

As I look back on some thirty years in the "dog game," I wonder how I made it from the stumbling novice, to the journeyman exhibitor, to the blase Specials owner, to the exalted ranks of judging. Certainly there was no plan. Only by being tenacious and by asking questions of everyone in sight did I finally "arrive."

In *The Great American Dog Show Game* I have attempted to impart some of the knowledge I have gained. To make it easy to absorb, I have used levity and cartoons. However, the subject matter is important. Read it and become a knowledgeable dog person. Best of all, enjoy it.

A.G.

Contents

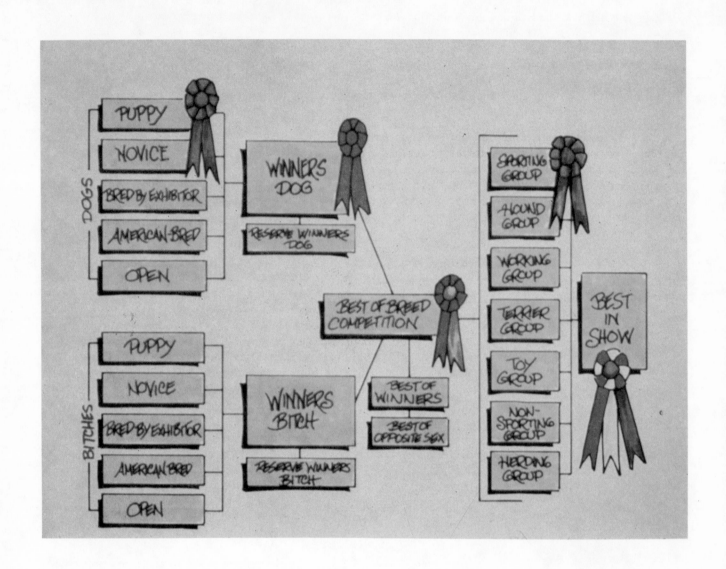

Getting Started in Purebred Dogs

It was a lovely summer evening. We had attended a late Saturday afternoon matinee at the theater in our local mall and were sauntering leisurely along, just window shopping. And there in the window of a newly opened pet shop was a litter of adorable puppies. They were so cute and funny as they tumbled about, each one trying to be fierce and serious. Then their unsteady feet slipped out from under them and they collapsed in a heap, taking their pride down with them. We must have watched them for half an hour before grinning at each other and moving on.

When we got home we turned to each other and almost in unison said, "Let's get a puppy!" Old Fritz, our mixed breed, had been dead more than a year and as we had dried our tears over his death we had said never again. Now we were grinning like kids in anticipation of a new toy.

"Let's get a purebred this time," my wife, Grace, said.

"But aren't they awfully expensive?" I countered.

"But we could take pride in having a real pedigreed dog. Besides, why not?"

Now how could I argue with that logic? "Okay, how about going back and getting one of those puppies we saw in the window? They were really cute."

The next evening we were back at the pet store. Sure enough, there were still three puppies left, all females.

"But I want a male dog," I insisted. "Besides, I don't even know what breed they are."

"They're Keeshonden," said the man in the white coat, walking up beside us. "Real good dogs they are." Then he named a price. After I got up off the floor I pointed out that that was more than my whole week's salary.

Grace asked to see their papers.

"Well . . . ," said the man, "we'll send them along as soon as they arrive. These are genuine farm-raised Midwestern dogs."

"But they do have AKC papers?" I asked.

"Of course they do," he said. "They haven't come in yet from the breeders but as soon as they do you can be sure I will send them to you."

After a few more minutes of discussion we wandered out, promising to come back again after we discussed finances.

"Let's look somewhere else to get some comparison," said the spouse. "Besides, I never heard of a Keeshond. Is it purebred?"

"Sure," I said sagely, "of course it is."

"Well, where do you think we should look?"

"Hey, I know! Every weekend the local kennel club runs an ad in the classified section. Let's call them!" And that's what we did, and it was the best decision we could have made.

The first thing the lady asked us when we called was what breed we had in mind. When I couldn't give her an answer she pointed out that there were well over one hundred breeds registered with The American Kennel Club. For the life of me I couldn't think of more than ten. Sensing my confusion, she graciously invited us to her house the next evening to discuss dogs in general and to help us secure the "right" puppy in particular.

"Let me show you this chart. You see the majority of dogs are in the middle. Most point winners, and the majority of finishable dogs, come from the above-average category, about sixteen percent.

"The top contenders for Best-of-Breed honors come from the superior group comprising some six percent.

"The top-winning Group and Best-in-Show dogs come from this final elite group that is made up of only two percent of the dog population."

Distribution of the Dog Population

Very Poor	2.2
Poor	6.7
Marginal	16.1
Average	50.0
Above Average	16.1
Superior	6.7
Very Superior	2.2

Arriving at her home we found it to be a model for small breeders. Part of the garage had been soundproofed and turned into a kennel, with runs extending out from the garage into the back yard. The runs were fenced with chain link and had a gravel surface. They were clean and had no odor. Mrs. Bostwick bred Boston Terriers and they were all anxious to greet us.

After serving us a cup of coffee Mrs. Bostwick brought out the AKC book which described all the breeds and included pictures. Some I had never seen. There was a Saluki, a Welsh Corgi, a Bichon, and a Pomeranian. We were amazed to learn that members of the local kennel club bred, showed, and offered for sale over sixty different breeds. Having been a successful breeder for over twenty years, Mrs. Bostwick was a veritable fountain of knowledge.

She began by saying, "Buying a purebred dog is not necessarily a guarantee that you are buying a 'show' dog. However, a purebred dog from a breeder and club member is in itself a guarantee of a healthy dog of good bloodlines that would be able to reproduce its breed type. Now, not all people buy a dog for showing. Are you interested in a show specimen?"

"What's the difference between a show specimen and just a purebred dog?" I asked.

"Well, a show specimen adheres more closely to the breed Standard and is of excellent conformation. It's not easy to consistently breed good show dogs. For example, did you know that only about two percent of all the dogs bred are of high enough quality to be Best-in-Show dogs? An important point needs to be made here. Not all dogs are show winners. The majority are just average. Perhaps only about twenty-five percent of all dogs bred for show really ever make it in the show ring.

Since Mrs. Bostwick seemed to be just warming to her task, we sat back and listened.

"You know, just being involved in some phase of breeding or showing appeals to some types of people more than to others. Usually that is true for those who are competitive and creative in nature." (The wife and I just looked at each other and grinned—that's us she's talking about!) Mrs. Bostwick went on, "It is my experience that most successful breeders are artistic to some degree, and have an ability to perceive space/depth relationships. It also pays to be intelligent, for breeding is a creative art whereby the breeder fashions his 'ideal' dog based upon a mental image of perfection."

Grace sensed the time was ripe to tell Mrs. Bostwick about her training as a painter at the Chicago Art Institute. "Great!" said Mrs. Bostwick. As she looked quizzically at me I was forced to confess that I couldn't draw a straight line—but competitive, that I was!

"Good again," said Mrs. Bostwick. "The competitive spirit in showing dogs can serve as a great motivator for constant improvement of your stock, when channeled in the right direction."

This gal seemed to know what she was talking about so I asked her how we should go about becoming breeders and getting into this dog show game. Well, she must have liked us because she gave us some very valuable advice, without which we never would have made it in the dog game.

"First," she said, "pay no attention to most of the books which advise the budding novice to obtain the very best bitch he can afford and proceed from that point with a sound, well-thought-out breeding program. My experience is that it seldom works out that way.

"To begin with there is the question of what constitutes a good bitch. Second, there is the problem of where you could find such a good bitch for sale. Obviously, an experienced and successful breeder is not likely to sell a good bitch from producing bloodlines to a complete novice. That breeder, if he has a surplus of such bitches at all, is looking to place that bitch with experienced breeders where her potential can be realized and her show and producing ability will reflect positively on the kennel where she was bred. Breeders have learned through sad experience that this seldom happens with novice owners."

We nodded our heads at each other. That sounded like good advice. Again Grace spoke up, saying, "Sure, you're right. How could people like us who can't even tell one breed from another be expected to develop and follow through with a sound, well-thought-out breeding program at this stage of the game?"

You know, I was real proud of that gal. She has a good head on her shoulders.

Mrs. Bostwick sat there rocking back and forth, sizing us up. I could almost see the wheels going round and round in her head.

"You know, by advising everyone to start with that bitch, the assumption is made that everyone wants to be and is cut out to be a breeder. That is *not true!* I can almost tell in advance a person's probability of success as a breeder."

I thought maybe she was crystal-ball gazing, but I was brought up to be polite, so I piped up and asked, "How can you do that?"

"Simple. There are certain abilities that enable some people to achieve a greater degree of success than others. For example, there are those who have an innate 'eye' for a dog and therefore have an easier time understanding the various abstract concepts of breeding, such as symmetry and balance. As I mentioned earlier, breeders attempt to fashion their ideal dog based upon their own mental concept of the Standard of their breed. If that picture in their head isn't clear, then they cannot possibly translate it into reality. They often breed dogs that emphasize excellence in some specific feature, but their dogs will lack a certain cohesive whole. Namely, the dogs are not put together so that the parts flow together and complement and strengthen each other.

"Unfortunately, there are some extremely knowledgeable breeders who have never been able to bring it off. They can talk a great dog, but they are not able to produce outstanding specimens.

"Well, here I am running on again. How about some more coffee? No? *Well,* just so I wouldn't bore you to tears I have invited one of the top Cocker Spaniel breeders in the country to come over this evening to give you the benefit of his experience. His name is James Hallway and he is the President of our local kennel club. He should be here in a few minutes. Are there any questions you want to ask me before he arrives?"

"Um, yes," I said, "there is. Can we expect to buy a good show dog from any member of the local club?"

Mrs. Bostwick chuckled, and said, "I'll let Mr. Hallway answer that one."

Mr. Hallway showed up just after nine o'clock, and after having a stiff bourbon was ready to talk dogs. (I wondered if, after I became a successful breeder, I would be offered a stiff bourbon.) I repeated my earlier question and watched the look he passed to Mrs. Bostwick. "That's not an easy question to answer," he hedged. "Let me try to tackle it this way.

"It's amazing how many people expect to be able to purchase good dogs from sources which have not proven themselves to be successful in producing good dogs. One reason is that it doesn't take much—perhaps a few blue ribbons and some puppy match trophies—to convince the average beginner that he or she is dealing with the greatest and most successful of breeders.

"Now, I will give you a few good rules of thumb to use in selecting a breeder to buy from. First, buy from a breeder who is well established and has been successful. Any breeder's reputation can be judged by objective criteria; mainly, what has he accomplished during his career as a breeder? Have his dogs finished their championships with good show records and among good competition? Does he sell his dogs to others or does he keep them for himself? Are his dogs and their bloodlines in demand? Are they 'producing' lines? Do others breed to his dogs?" He talked a mile a minute, and I got writer's cramp trying to take notes and keep up.

"Do you have any other questions?"

"Yes," sang out Grace. "Even after we select a puppy, how can we tell if we are on the right track?"

"Good question," said Mrs. Bostwick.

"Agreed," said Mr. Hallway, "and I think I can give you some guidance in that department. It is very important to the eventual success of a beginner to form a good relationship with a successful and knowledgeable breeder from whom the beginner can learn many different things. I don't mean to imply that this relationship would discourage independent thought and action on your part, but rather that it should supplement your own thoughts and contribute to your growth. Don't forget that breeding is an art which requires much thought, study, understanding, and perception. The beginner needs to be encouraged, as you are tonight, to ask questions, and to sift the facts out of much advice and many opinions that will be offered. You need to develop an 'eye' for your breed and keep adding to your experience. You're not gifted with these insights overnight, and you need to acquire this information from others who have been over the route before.

"So the first step in a breeding program is to select a breed you would enjoy living with. Have you one in mind?"

"No, not yet, but we know what we like," I said.

"Okay, let's see if we can narrow it down further," said Jim. (I call people I like by their first name.) "What size dog do you want to own?"

"Well, taller than your Bostons or Cockers, but not as tall as a Doberman."

"What kind of coat?"

"Not heavy . . . easy to brush, I guess."

"Would the dog live indoors?"

"No, we would like a rugged type of dog that could live

in a dog house outside and come in and out."

"Do you have exercise space?"

"Yes, we have a good-sized yard."

"Should it like kids?"

"That's not important, since we don't have any, but I would like it to be a friendly dog."

"How about a watchdog personality?"

"No. It should be alert and bark at strangers, but we don't want a guard dog."

"Any color preference?"

"Brownish, white, gray—any of those are okay."

After further narrowing down our preferences and looking in the AKC dog book, we came up with the Norwegian Elkhound, the fifteen-inch Beagle, and the Siberian Husky.

After discussing the pros and cons of those three breeds we focused on the Husky as our choice. Now where would we find the right one? As luck would have it, Mr. Hallway was acquainted with a top breeder who lived in an adjacent state and within reasonable driving distance. As he recalled, she had a young litter that looked quite good. Bingo—we were on our way.

Thursday night found us in Weaverville to look at that promising litter. The breeder, Mrs. Moneypenny, was most gracious. In her grooming area she had many ribbons tacked to the wall. Many said "Best of Breed" and "Best of Winners"; anyway, they looked impressive. But the most impressive thing of all was a huge silver punch bowl which she said had been won recently by the sire of the litter we were to see. I figured anyone who could accumulate almost as much silver as the Hunt brothers must have good dogs.

The litter was four months old and each of the five puppies impressed me. There were two bitches and three dogs. We had already decided to get a male, so we studied those three most carefully. This one guy was a real kick.

He was definitely the king of the mountain. Mrs. Moneypenny also had an older litter with two good males in it and we saw them as well. Hm, pretty nice dogs. We asked her advice on which one to choose.

"Basically, a young puppy is less expensive than an older puppy," she said. "But you should understand that by obtaining a younger one you are taking more risks. If the puppy matures with the quality indicated by its early promise, then you have made a good bargain. On the other hand, should some serious fault appear that was not apparent at an early age, such as second teeth coming in bad, then you are stuck with a faulty specimen on which you have wasted time, effort, and money, to say nothing of your emotional involvement and perhaps a stymied breeding program. A larger sum spent in the beginning on an older puppy often proves to be the cheapest in the long run.

"Frankly," Mrs. Moneypenny said, "you can do better, quality-wise, by buying a male as your first dog to show."

"Why's that?" Grace asked.

"Well, like most breeders, I keep very few males, and then only if they are 'Specials' quality." Not wanting to appear ignorant, I sagely nodded my head—but what was a 'Special'? Fortunately she went on to enlighten us. "Specials dogs are those that not only finish their championships easily but also go on to win Groups and Best in Shows.

"Now this older puppy appears to be extremely good, but I can't keep him because I have his full brother from another litter. To get him into a home where he would be loved and shown, I would let him go now at a reasonable price."

And so it came to pass that we became the proud owners of a seven-month-old Siberian Husky.

Our First Dog Show

We were about to embark on one of the great adventures of our lives. We learned that the dog show "game" can become an all-consuming passion for some and an interesting hobby for most. You would not be reading this book if your interest hadn't already been stimulated.

So whether your chosen breed is Poodle or Chihuahua, your adventures will be relatively the same. We found out that before starting off on any adventure it's a wise idea to have a map of the terrain and a clear idea of the rules of the game. Like many, we were a bit perplexed by some of the terms we heard bandied about, such as "Winners," "slipped stifles," "grizzle colored," "single tracking," "dysplasia," "Best of Opposite Sex." These terms and many others are the language of the dog game. Don't worry—like us, you will learn more about these terms as you go along. They are just a few of the things we learned about the "business" of registering and exhibiting purebred dogs.

First, to give you an idea of how vast the game is, let us start with some statistics. There are now 128 breeds recognized by The American Kennel Club, the regulatory body overseeing the dog game in the United States. Most breeds come to us from foreign shores. There are few native American breeds. In 1984 there were about a thousand all breed shows held in the United States and some fourteen hundred Specialty shows. All breed shows are events put on by local kennel clubs under the sanction of the AKC and generally have classes for all breeds of dogs. A Specialty show, on the other hand, is put on by a single breed club (for example, the Podunk Poodle Club), and the event is sanctioned by both the national, or parent, club of the breed and by the AKC. The Specialty shows are for only one breed.

Organizing, supervising, and regulating the far-flung activity is The American Kennel Club, with offices at 51 Madison Avenue in New York City. The AKC is a private corporation established under the laws of the State of New York. Its primary functions are:

—Registration of purebred dogs.

—Publication of a stud register.

—Keeping and publishing statistics through the *American Kennel Gazette,* its monthly magazine.

—Recognizing new dog clubs as show-giving entities under AKC development rules.

—Educating the public through publications, seminars, and audio-visual media.

—Sponsorship of research into major medical and physical problems of dogs.

—Sanctioning dates and places for dog clubs to hold their shows.

—Providing oversight of the shows themselves through AKC field representatives.

—Licensing of judges to officiate at AKC-approved events.

—Supplying U.S. representatives to international bodies interested in promoting the sport of purebred dogs.

The AKC is governed by a body of delegates, each nominated by his or her local kennel club or the parent club of a breed, and approved by the delegates themselves. A Board of Directors is chosen from among the delegates, some of whom in turn appoint those officers who run the organization on a day-to-day basis.

To be entered in a regular dog show or obedience trial, your dog must be eligible to be registered with the AKC. Otherwise, your dog cannot be shown.

Let's see how the process works. Just as we purchased our Husky puppy, you may purchase a purebred dog from a reputable breeder and be given the registration papers. You need to fill them out, listing two choices for names you would like your dog to have. Sign the papers, attach your check, and get them into the mail pronto. The AKC asks for two choices of names because so many people choose the same names, so don't be surprised if the registration certificate comes back with your second choice, as ours did—King Rudolph XII. Once you have received this registration certificate, your dog is registered. This is no guarantee of quality, but only means that your dog has AKC's stamp that it is purebred. The *quality* label is what dog *shows* are all about.

Now, lo and behold, your puppy is growing up and looks like a world beater to you. All your friends tell you that you should show him. Great! Where do you get started?

Most local kennel clubs and Specialty clubs hold what are known as sanctioned matches. These are simulated dog shows where puppies and their owners can become acclimated to the dog show world under "play" conditions. Awards are given, but the wins do not count toward AKC championship points. The judges are usually local breeders, professional handlers, or licensed AKC judges who are seeking to be sanctioned for judging additional breeds. The judges, exhibitors, and handlers use this type of show to "try their wings." It's a great training ground.

I alluded to AKC championship points, so I'll discuss those next. It takes fifteen points to become a champion. Here is how your dog earns them. The first step is entering your dog in a regular AKC all-breed or Specialty show. The classes provided are:

—Puppy—over six months and under nine months.

—Puppy—over nine months but under twelve months.

—Novice—has not won a blue ribbon.

—Bred by exhibitor—you must have bred and currently own the dog in order to show in this class.

—American-bred—must have been bred in the United States.

—Open Class—all comers.

—Specials—champions only.

(In certain Specialty shows puppy classes may be extended to eighteen months of age.)

Rudolph was over ten months of age when we got ready to show him. We thought it best to enter him in the nine to twelve month class. We found out that since Rudolph was a male, he would face only males in his class. (The dog game is still chauvinistic.) There are separate paths to the top for dogs and bitches, each entered in classes with identical names and restrictions.

To enter your dog in a show you need to obtain an entry form from your local dog club or from a licensed show superintendent. You can get the addresses of show superintendents from any breeder. After securing the entry form, fill it out, enclose a check for the proper amount, and get it into the mail before the stated deadline. You will now be on a mailing list. You may never get *off* that mailing list!

Next, we were told to make sure we had the proper grooming tools to prepare Rudolph for the big day. We

checked with an experienced breeder about getting Rudolph trimmed. The first few times we paid another experienced person to groom him while we observed. Then we took a stab at it on our own. If you choose this route be sure to ask why your dog is to be trimmed a certain way.

We were advised that it also wouldn't hurt to leash train and practice posing Rudolph in the back yard. We also took him for walks at the local shopping center, where there were crowds of people, to get him used to people and noise.

The week of our first show we received a notice from the show superintendent giving us our entry number, the time of showing, and the judge of our breed. Directions to the show were included.

Came the dawn of the big day and we hopped out of bed at 6:00 a.m. for the forty-five minute ride to the show, where Rudolph was slated to be shown at 1:30 p.m. Don't want to be late, do we? Since Rudolph was our only dog we didn't feel we needed one of those kennel boxes we had seen. Besides, he would rather ride in Grace's lap. New show lead, comb, brush, dog cookies, all in order. Off we went, onto the expressway and on to the Greater Flim Flam Kennel Club Show held at Trancas Corners in Onetta.

As we approached Onetta, population 3,500, we saw on a telephone pole a sign that read "Dog Show," and an arrow pointing straight ahead. Off the freeway we went, looking for the next sign. There it is! A quick right turn, and ten minutes later there was an eerie silence in the car as the cornfields whizzed by. This did not look like the way to a dog show. So we turned around and headed back.

"Hey, there's someone with a dog crate in his station wagon," I shouted. "Let's follow him, he must know where he's going." Ten minutes later and more cornfields and the guy in front of us stopped and got out. So did we. When we compared notes we found out it was his first show too, and he had never been near the place.

Back we went to the expressway and the original sign. By the time we got there, there were four other cars clustered around it. Everyone was lost! Welcome to the world of dog shows. Just then a long-haired kid on a motorcycle cruised by and said he would lead us to the show site.

Sure enough, just off the next exit was the fairgrounds, and more cars than I'd seen since the last Rams football game. As we eased our car off the expressway we joined a long line of cars waiting to get into the parking lot.

After fifteen minutes, we crept up to the entrance. In front of us materialized a man with a change apron on, telling us, "It's a buck and a half to park." We forked over the money, drove two feet, and another guy stopped us and told us it was three more bucks for a catalog. We didn't

know a catalog from Adam's off ox, but we figured buying it was the thing to do. Finally, when it seemed as if we had driven ten miles over the ruts, some other guy wildly waved us to our parking spot. We had arrived.

All around us there seemed to be organized chaos. Dogs were barking, little kids were chasing other little kids, and everyone had at least one dog. Some dogs were on show leads, like ours, others were in crates which were stacked on dollies and were being pushed and pulled along. We joined the exodus from the parking lot and, after what seemed like a twenty mile hike, arrived at the entrance to the show grounds. There, another officious individual asked for our Exhibitors Pass. That was what we had gotten in the mail. In we went. We had entered a land and an adventure that would change our whole life.

We went looking for ring 12 and Judge Figuero Rollins. Would it be indoors or outdoors? There was ring 12 on the other side of the field! Over we went, threading our way between rings and seeing breeds we never knew existed. Golden Retrievers, Irish Wolfhounds, Bernese Mountain Dogs. Wow! Finally we arrived at ring 12 and there was a Mr. Fred Dicey judging a big hairy breed. Where were Judge Rollins and the Siberian Huskys? We asked a lady who had a badge on that read "Committee," and she pointed out that it was only 11:30 and Judge Rollins was not due in that ring to judge Huskys until 1:30 p.m. Until then Mr. Dicey would go happily on judging Newfoundlands. Oh, so *that's* what those were.

"Okay gang," I yelled, "let's go have lunch! I smell onions, so there must be a hamburger stand around."

Soon it was 1:15 and time to get back to ring 12. My word, where did all those Huskys come from? According to the catalog there were six other puppies in our class. Boy they looked good! The steward called the class, and was I *scared*—if it hadn't been for Rudolph pulling on the lead I don't think my legs would have moved.

Were we lucky! Rudolph waltzed around the ring and even posed properly. And the judge, that admirable and highly intelligent man, pointed to him for first place over the six other puppies. I knew all along he could do it. (So why were my palms so sweaty?) The ring steward (the guy who gave me an arm band with a number on it and pointed the way into the ring) told me to stay close to the ring for "Winners." I watched as each of the other classes was judged and a winner selected for each, and then I was pushed back into the ring to compete with all those other winners. This was getting to be serious stuff. Once again that distinguished man (he must really have been an expert in my breed) pointed to us and said *Winners*— F-A-N-T-A-S-T-I-C! Rudolph was now the best male. Again the steward told me to stay close since we had to go back to compete for Best of Winners (what's that?) and Best of Breed.

I watched as the judge went through the same ritual in all the bitch classes, and lo and behold he selected one for Winners Bitch. I knew we had won Winners Dog, so there had to be two Winners. Then as I watched, the judge called the second place Open Bitch into the ring (the Winners Bitch, unlike Rudolph, had come from the Open Class) and now judged the second place bitch against all the other class winners. He even gave her Reserve Winners. (What's that?) I didn't remember seeing that happen in the Dog Class—of course, from way up there on cloud nine it was kind of hard to see what else happened after we had won.

I found out later that reserve, or runner-up, was important in case the winner was later disqualified on various and sundry technical points, for example, too old for its class or improperly entered, and that the reserve winner would then be entitled to the championship points earned by the disqualified dog. Okay, so Rudolph was Winners Dog—how many points did he win? Wouldn't it be nice if it were all fifteen and I wouldn't have to get so nervous again? The breeder of my puppy, Mrs. Moneypenny, was there, and oh so proud of him. She explained to me there was no way Rudolph could get all fifteen points in one fell swoop. The most he could earn was five at a time. That number was called a major win (most often just a major), as were wins of three and four points. I asked her how they were determined. Flipping to the first pages of the show catalog, she showed me the point scale for all the breeds. She explained that the scale was based on show entries from the previous year in that geographical area. Each breed has a different scale of points. I eagerly looked up Winners Dog. There it was, fourteen dogs, two points. Well, not fifteen at once, but a start.

Just as I was resigned to settle for my two points, Mrs. Moneypenny told me that there were four points in bitches, and that if my dog defeated the Winners Bitch for Best of Winners he would earn four points, a major no less, instead of two. She also pointed out that a dog had to earn two major wins among its fifteen points and they could not be awarded by the same judge. I was elated by the possibility, but then I thought, "Oh, no! If Rudolph wins, the Winners Bitch won't get any points. That's not fair." When I spoke this aloud Mrs. Moneypenny grinned and assured me the bitch wouldn't suffer. Both dogs would win four points. Now that's what I call a *great* system.

In we went for Best of Breed competition, and sure enough there were all the champions (would my little dog ever grow up to look like that?) and the Winners Bitch. After much soul-searching, the judge awarded a beautiful dog Best of Breed, Rudolph Best of Winners, and gave a bitch an award called Best of Opposite Sex—opposite of the sex that won, I cleverly guessed.

I learned that the awards were First through Fourth in each class (except Specials, where only a Best of Breed is given), and Winners and Reserve Dog and Winners and Reserve Bitch, as well as Best of Winners.

You might say I was hooked right then and there. This was the real stuff! I needed to know what was next on the agenda. The owner of the BOB dog told me that the next step in the show was for dogs which were the Best of Breed and Best of Variety (some breeds are subdivided by color, size, or type of coat) to compete with each other by Groups. The explanation was very complicated, so let me show you how it works. Here is a "map" that shows how you get from your class all the way to Best in Show. There are seven Groups divided roughly by function. They are:

I—Sporting—primarily bird dogs.

II—Hounds—primarily trailers, diggers, and hunters.

III—Working—primarily working, pulling, and guard dogs.

IV—Terriers—primarily bred to kill fox and vermin.

V—Toys—primarily small pet dogs.

VI—Non-Sporting—primarily a catch-as-catch-can grouping.

VII—Herding—primarily herding dogs.

As you can see, the winner of each of the seven Groups then comes in to compete for Best in Show. In the Group competition itself, the judges award First through Fourth place ribbons just as they did in the Puppy Class and all other classes.

Next I wanted to know when the Group competition began. I was told any time in the late afternoon, depending upon when the various judges finished judging dogs belonging to a specific Group. The show superintendent can usually tell from each judge's entry, because a licensed AKC judge is supposed to judge between twenty and twenty-five dogs an hour, and they are allowed by AKC rules to judge only 175 dogs at one show.

Since we had some time to kill before the first Group was scheduled to start, we decided to wander around the show grounds and see the sights.

The first thing that struck us was the number of vendors, selling everything from dog food to sleeping pads. The dog books attracted us first. What an assortment! My lord, there is more stuff published about dogs than I would ever need to know! We wound up buying a book about Huskys. As we stood there a lady came over with the longest dog I had ever seen. It was a Skye Terrier.

Next we wandered over to look at the dog statuettes. What beautiful art work. They looked almost real. Some people really knew about dog construction. This time we bought a beautiful Husky ceramic. Whew! I wondered if I would have enough money left for lunch on Monday. Just then we saw the breed of dog that is on the label of a famous Scotch whiskey. I was told it was a West Highland White Terrier and not a white Scottie, as I called it.

On to the grooming equipment and the dog toys booths. What a collection of stuff! I'd love to buy and buy. Maybe next time.

"Hey, what are all those vehicles doing over there close to the rings?" asked Grace. "Let's wander over and see. Have you ever seen so many motor homes and vans?" They looked like a gypsy caravan. "That guy over there checking his dogs near his motor home—he might know."

Yep, turned out he was a professional handler and he sure did know all about most everything that was connected with dog shows. It seems there is a select group of professionals who make their living training, grooming, and showing dogs. Some of them attend more than seventy-five shows a year. The "rigs," as the vehicles are called, are used by handlers and exhibitors alike. The larger ones generally belong to the professional handlers. Usually they pull into the showgrounds the night before a show. Show-giving clubs reserve space upon request and charge for setting up this area and allowing for the advantageous location.

Generally, members of this "gypsy caravan" are pretty well self-contained. They eat and sleep in their rigs and most have special setups for the dogs. Many have awnings to shield owners and dogs from the hot sun. The grooming and exercise areas are set up directly adjacent to each rig. Many vehicles have auxiliary generators so owners can generate their own electricity and air conditioning as needed without running the motor on the vehicle. The caravan area looked like a small portable city, ready to move on a moment's notice. In fact, it reminded me of the way a circus sets up and moves.

Just as I was envisioning myself in the driver's seat of one of those gigantic land cruisers, the announcer cut in to call out the first two Groups. It was to be Sporting first and Terriers second. Boy, there was sure a flurry of activity in the handlers' area as everyone got ready to rush off to the rings.

Since Rudolph was a Working Dog, we sashayed over to watch how the Husky BOB winner would make out against all the other dogs. The Working Group was to be the fourth Group judged.

I swear, there were dogs in the Sporting Group that I had never seen and never would have believed to exist. The Clumber Spaniel—if I hadn't been told differently, I would have sworn it couldn't hunt. The Field Spaniel looked like a mix of many of the Spaniels.

They all paraded into the ring, the bigger ones in front. Hey, did you know there is a Welsh Springer Spaniel? There is also an English Cocker Spaniel. Where did all these breeds come from?

Mrs. Moneypenny sat with us at ringside. She told us the judge was not necessarily comparing dogs with one another, but was primarily looking at how close each dog came to its own breed Standard. I was told that because there are so many top-flight dogs in the Group, it takes about half an hour to judge each Group. Finally the judge chose the Clumber for the number one spot.

The Terriers were next and a small red dog won (I was told later it was a Lakeland Terrier).

We waited around until the other four Groups were done. (The Herding Group had not been created at that time. As of January 1, 1983, the Working Group was divided and the Herding Group formed, comprised of fourteen breeds formerly classified as Working Breeds.) The winner of the Toy Group was a Silky Terrier; the Working Group was won by a Doberman Pinscher; the Non-Sporting Group by a Standard Poodle; and the Hound Group winner was a Norwegian Elkhound.

Now the call went out to get the Best in Show entries ready. In they came, all groomed to the teeth and showing their stuff. There was much applause as the judge stepped in to begin the tough task of picking the finalist. As each dog gaited individually, there was concentrated applause from its ringside supporters. The judge gaited and surveyed each one and after much consideration pointed to the Lakeland Terrier for Best in Show. You know, that dog got the least applause when he gaited. I guessed it wasn't a popularity contest.

It was six o'clock and we were bushed. Rudolph had been sleeping in a friend's crate for most of the afternoon and felt imposed upon when we woke him up to go home.

So a long but exciting day ended for us all. However, from what we learned that day we hoped there would be many, many more. I hope all of you will feel the same way.

Choosing a Professional Handler

During the two weeks after Rudolph's historic win, the ribbons and photographs were shown over and over again to everyone in the neighborhood and at my office. In fact, the staff was ducking when I came around to tell again of Rudolph's moment of triumph.

We read the Husky book we purchased at the show from cover to cover—*twice*. It was clear to us that Rudolph could become one of the immortals of the breed. After all, his father and mother were champions and his ancestors were described in glowing terms in the book.

We went to visit Mrs. Moneypenny, the breeder. "Is it true we have a world beater sleeping on our bed?" we asked her.

"Well, yes and no," said Mrs. Moneypenny. (Now you can tell by that answer that she is a wise old breeder.) "Rudolph was a very promising puppy. If he continues to develop as he has, he could become an outstanding show dog. However, if you want him to have a great show career he must be shown to his full advantage—and frankly, neither of you is experienced enough to do this." Mrs. Moneypenny explained that she was too busy to make many of the shows herself so she couldn't do it either. "Of course, there *is* a way, if you want to use a professional handler."

We immediately flashed back to the show two weeks before and our visit to the handler's area.

"Now that's not a bad idea!"

"But poor Rudolph would have to ride caged up in one of those crates and he would miss us," cried the wife.

"No, no, no," insisted Mrs. Moneypenny. "That's not so. Handlers take dogs as 'ringside pickups.' That is, they will accept a dog that the owner brings to the show himself. However, before we get into a big long discussion, let me tell you what a handler is, what he does, and what he can do for you.

"First of all, handlers have an association of their own known as the Professional Handlers' Association. The majority belong to this group. Its members usually wear a PHA pin at the shows so that they can be recognized. The PHA is an organization of handlers dedicated to the purpose of representing handlers for the betterment of dog activities throughout the country. They distribute information on better business practices, have a code of ethics, and serve as a coordinating and information source. They attempt to maintain and improve good relationships between the handlers and their clients and between handlers and The American Kennel Club.

"Most handlers started out just as you are doing now. My own handler was a postman who showed his and other people's dogs on weekends until he felt he had become experienced enough to go into handling full time. Most handlers were breeders first and learned the ins and outs of the dog game over many years before becoming full time professional handlers. Others, after gaining such experience, become judges.

"At first, most handlers specialize in the breed they bred, and then branch out. Many still specialize in dogs of a certain Group. For example, some of the country's top handlers handle nothing but Terriers. On the other hand, my handler has handled to Best in Show a Dachshund from the Hound Group, a Springer from the Sporting Group, and a Doberman from the Working Group.

"Another way to become a good handler is to become an apprentice or assistant to a handler. In this capacity you assist the handler in kennel care, grooming, getting dogs to and from the show ring, and are a general handyperson. If you will observe at your next show, most handlers have such assistants. Some with large strings of dogs will have a number of assistants.

"After serving in this capacity for a number of years and becoming fully trained, the assistants usually branch out on their own. This apprenticeship system has worked well and many of our current handlers came up that way."

"Okay, okay, we're convinced. How do we go about finding the right handler for Rudolph, and what does it cost?" I asked Mrs. Moneypenny.

She thought for a few minutes and then painted the picture for us. "Naturally," she said, "your priority in what is best for your dog may be different from mine. I can only comment on what I feel is relevant and convey my views in the hope that they might be of interest and value to you.

"Hiring a handler costs hard-earned money. Therefore, you should compare handler's fees. This financial aspect should be discussed first because many people think immediately, how much money is this going to cost? However, be forewarned—don't allow a little more expense to sway a decision on your choice of the right handler. You generally get what you pay for. You must

remember that it is not solely the handling service in the show ring for which you are billed. Good kennel facilities, comfortable, safe transportation, and reliable and responsible help at the kennel and on the road don't come cheaply, and all are important factors to be considered.

"Any handler would like to be chosen as a true professional. If he or she looks and acts the part, it's a plus. Anyone who is slovenly or dirty in his or her appearance might very easily and often unconsciously allow the dogs to look the same, so choose a handler who has apparent respect for clean habits.

"Select a handler who is ethical and whose business practices are sound. Clients become justifiably dissatisfied when financial arrangements are vague, so be sure to have an equally sound, businesslike attitude when you approach any handler and ask for a rate card. Be prepared to fill out a client-handler contract. In this way you and the handler will have a clear understanding of how the business relationship will be conducted. While you are dealing with finances, it would be advisable to determine whether the handler is financially able to pay for emergency veterinary services which might have to be dealt with on an out-of-town trip.

"It is said that winning is the name of the game. In any sport, a competitive attitude with a strong emphasis on details is a winning one. Choose a handler who hopefully will win for you as often and as consistently as possible in a sportsmanlike manner without having to resort to devious means in or out of the ring. Select a handler with integrity—one who is beyond reproach and one who is impeccable in character. Far better to aim high! Most importantly, remember your handler is your representative in the ring and his actions are reflective of you.

"In choosing a handler, be judicious with respect to specialization. For example, since you own a Husky, select a handler who is knowledgeable about the Working breeds and who can 'put the dog down' to perfection. We live in an age of specialization and the dog game is no exception. All these factors, together with the art of grooming and presenting the dog to its very best advantage, add up to first-class service—the very thing you are seeking! You may want your handler to be an advisor in your breeding program too, so if this is the case, select one who has an understanding of Huskys and who may have first-hand knowledge of bloodlines, which could prove most valuable. Here you will need to trust him too, so again his honesty and integrity are going to be important.

"There are many basic parts which together make the whole relationship a successful union. Each is as important in its own way as you want it to be. A truly successful and long-lasting business relationship is not impossible to achieve if you approach an honest handler you can admire and trust. The other part of a successful relationship is unquestionably between handler and dog.

This relationship alone will be the final test of whether your choice was the right one.

"Your best bet is to narrow down the list of handlers to those who are in the area and who have had successful experiences in handling Siberian Huskys and know the breed. Then go to the shows and watch these people at work. When you have satisfied yourself that they can do the job, make an opportunity to talk to them and learn specifically their method of operation and the exact charges for their services."

Leaving Mrs. Moneypenny's kennel we resolved to look through the handlers sections in various magazines to see who lived in the area and specialized in our breed. Some faces came to mind from the win photographs we had been looking at recently.

After days of poring over *Kennel Review, Dog World,* and other magazines, we had boiled our list down to three handlers who lived within three hundred miles and attended most of the shows in our area. We decided to go to the Oakmont Kennel Club Show the following Saturday and watch the three in action before talking to them.

After arriving at Oakmont we checked the rings and breeds our potential handlers were committed to for the day. We agreed that Ladislaus Swiftworthy would be first in ring 6 handling Poodles, then John Trumpeter in ring 1 with Afghans, and finally Lydia Axelrod in ring 8 with Golden Retrievers.

As we approached ring 6, the dogs and handlers were waiting to go into the ring. We observed Ladislaus combing his dog and getting ready. We watched attentively as he set his entry down inside the ring and posed it for the judge. The dog seemed well trained, clean, and well groomed. As he gaited the dog he seemed to move it slower for the side view than going away from the judge. We wondered why. He didn't win the class, placing third,

but since we knew nothing about Poodles, we couldn't tell if his dog was deserving or not.

Off we went to observe John Trumpeter. The first thing that impressed us was that John was a fashion plate. I wondered how he could work that hard and still look as if he had just stepped out of the shower. We decided that John was not going to be our cup of tea. Nothing definite. We just felt something. We figured if the chemistry wasn't right we wouldn't pursue it.

So it was on to observe Lydia with Goldens. She was smartly turned out in a sensible outfit that allowed her maximum freedom of movement. We liked her style. She handled her dogs with a crispness and sure-handedness that we liked. Besides, she won!

"Okay, it's Lydia and Ladislaus. Let's see if we can get to talk to them when they have a bit of time between rings," I said.

We wandered out to where the handlers' rigs were parked. There we saw everything from modified trucks to recreational vehicles to converted vans. The handlers' area was fascinating for us novices. We had visited the area briefly at our first show, but this time we were determined to do an in-depth inspection of the rigs and equipment.

Inside the rigs there was a variety of housing conditions for the dogs. Most had an area for stacking the crates. The dogs seemed quite comfortable in their homes away from home. We liked the easy camaraderie of the handlers' quarters. The handlers all knew each other and seemed to help the other guy out in a pinch. That made us feel good.

We talked to a handler's client who had come out to check on her dog right after it had won the breed. She was delighted with her dog but was concerned about how long she could continue to campaign it. Inflation was cutting into her spendable income. Hmm, that's one we'll have to think about.

18

At two o'clock we had a chance to talk to Ladislaus. He was a charming man who had been an engineer with an aerospace company when the country was riding the space boom. When things got tight, he saw the handwriting on the wall and switched to handling full time. He has never been sorry. He introduced us to his wife, Marion, who was his chief aide, and handled some dogs on her own. He said there were many such husband and wife teams. Their rig was a moderate-sized vehicle. Marion said they had set an upper limit of ten dogs that they would carry at one time. They also had agreed that they would not take more than three dogs as ringside pickups at each show, and then only if it did not conflict with their full-time dogs.

She went on to point out that they felt they could do a better job with a dog they had with them full-time, for these reasons:

—They would have better opportunities to get to know the dog and its personality traits.

—The dog would know them and be used to them and thus respond better in the ring.

—There would be time to train the dog to show to its potential.

—Grooming and bathing the dog properly before each weekend of shows would be their responsibility and they were professionals at the task.

—The dog would be properly conditioned, roadwork and all, and be in tip top shape.

Well, I must say that was all worth thinking about. Gingerly, I approached the topic of money. Ladislaus produced a rate card and said they would be willing to discuss their rates at length with us. First and foremost, he said, to show a class dog they charged a flat rate that included training and grooming. The flat rate included making the show entries and transporting the dog to and from the shows. Board was additional and based on the size of the dog. Any veterinary assistance was also an added cost. Ringside pickup was at a much reduced fee

and would include some touch-up grooming at the show.

However, and it was a big however, said Marion, all of this was predicated on their approval of Rudolph. She pointed out that they showed only dogs that were of quality and had a good chance of finishing their championships. Ladislaus chimed in to explain that to do otherwise would be taking our money under false pretenses. Both of us liked that approach. After more small talk we said goodbye to them and went to visit with Lydia.

On our way over we looked at each other and admitted we liked what we saw. They seemed to be ethical and competent professionals and came across well. Their dogs also looked as if they were well cared for and liked their handlers.

As we came upon Lydia's area, she was just putting a group of dogs out to exercise. Her rig was much larger than the Swiftworthys' and she had three assistants helping her. We were invited in for a cup of coffee while we talked. Inside the rig there was a nice living area to accommodate three people and a big area for the dog crates and paraphernalia. Lydia apologized for not seeing us sooner but explained that she had most of her entries between 10 a.m. and 1 p.m. that day.

We told her about Rudolph and what Mrs. Moneypenny had said and how we had boiled down our choices. She was very complimentary about Marion and Ladislaus and said they could do a fine job for us. This took us aback. The wife asked, "Aren't you interested in handling Rudolph?"

"Yes, of course I am," Lydia said. "But right now I am booked pretty solid. I probably couldn't get to Rudolph for at least another three months. Besides, why do you want to push a puppy so fast?" That was a new one on us. I guess we had figured you just went ahead and showed your dog any time.

Then Lydia explained about showing a dog when *it* was

ready and at its peak, and that a dog that wasn't mature and ready to go was just giving the judge an extra reason not to put him up.

We accepted that. "If you could take Rudolph, what would you charge?"

Like the Swiftworthys, she showed us her rate card and also a contract for services which spelled out to a gnat's eyebrow exactly what services she would be committed to perform and what was expected of us, as clients. She pointed out that this contract was based upon a model form put out by the Professional Handlers' Association.

Then Lydia brought up a matter that we hadn't even thought about. What if Rudolph turned out to be a super-dog who could finish his championship easily and could be a top Specials dog? What then? Were we prepared to go on or did we just want him to finish his championship? Oh boy, thoughts of sugarplum fairies and Best-in-Show wins danced through our heads. We were carried away. Before my wife could object I blurted out, "We want to go all the way!"

At that Lydia smiled, and said, "It isn't that easy, and it could cost you money you might not be willing to spend."

"Like what?" I asked.

"Well, for starters, I charge an extra fee for winning a Group and a lesser amount for placing. Additionally, there is an added charge if your dog goes Best in Show."

There I was, caught between my dreams of winning Best-in-Show awards and pleading poverty at the same time. After gulping two or three times, I said, "Well, that's food for thought." Just then my wife saved me from myself by jumping in and saying that we could continue this conversation the next week when we drove up to Lydia's kennel so she could appraise Rudolph's chances of being a truly big winner.

As we left Lydia's rig, I admit I was a bit green around the gills. I had almost spent money that I didn't have. On the other hand—oh well, I'll think about that later.

After dinner that night we decided to come to grips with our dilemma. Let's face it, Grace said, we are not the heirs to the Rockefeller fortune, nor can we afford to go into permanent debt to show the dog. Let's define exactly what we want to do and see if we can afford it.

This is what we came up with:

1. We would wait until Rudolph was fifteen months of age before we showed him again. This would allow him time to mature and give us time to save money over the next seven months for his show career.

2. We would ask our handler to go along with ringside pickup until Rudolph finished his championship.

3. With the money we had saved and the money we would earmark from our "extra fund," we would campaign Rudolph as a Special for six months to see how he would do.

Satisfied with those choices we now turned to deciding which handler we would use. Of course this was predicated upon the handler's accepting Rudolph. I was afraid to speak first for fear of disagreement, but the wife solved that problem. In the words of Solomon, she said, "I don't think there can be any disagreement if we choose the Swiftworthys." We called Lydia and cancelled our plans to see her again.

As a loyal husband, well versed in the logic of a woman's reasoning, I accepted her decision. Tell me, what would you have done?

Campaigning a Specials Dog

Well, eight months later Rudolph finished with a rush, capturing four majors, two Best of Breeds, and a Group Second. We were overwhelmed. The dog was sixteen months of age and in peak condition. The question was, now what?

Ladislaus and Marion, his handlers, thought they had a hot one on their hands and wanted to discuss long-range plans. We had been putting aside money which we saved by using ringside pickup and were contemplating our next steps. We decided to sit down and talk about the future, poorhouse or not.

"Never in my wildest dreams did I think our puppy would grow up like this," I said. "I hoped he would finish easily, but this is more than I was prepared for."

Grace smiled with contentment. "Yes," she said, "but wasn't it fun?" I had to agree that basking in the reflected light of a top winning dog was heady stuff indeed.

We had been welcomed and congratulated to a fare-thee-well. Everyone seemed to love Rudolph and wanted to offer suggestions on what to do next. Frankly, we were nonplused.

"I'm sure Ladislaus and Marion are sincere in wanting us to show Rudolph as a Special. But what does that entail? How should we go about it? How long should we show him? And what can we expect in the way of rewards?"

"Well," I said, taking the bull by the horns, "I'm going to telephone them and try to straighten out some of these problems."

First off, Ladislaus pointed out that Rudolph would be his number two call dog because he had a German Shorthaired Pointer as his number one dog.

"Whoa, hold on a minute," I pleaded. "What's a 'number two dog' mean?"

Ladislaus explained that the people who owned the Shorthair were senior to us as clients and he had been showing their dog for over a year as a Special.

"Yes," I said, "but how does that figure when the dogs don't compete in the same Group?"

He pointed out that at some shows two Groups are run at the same time. If this occurred, and both dogs had won their breeds, he was obligated to take in the German Shorthair. This would also be true in those cases when both dogs won their respective Groups. Of course, Marion

would take Rudolph on those occasions. Okay, that I could live with, for Marion had won with Rudolph already.

Marion got on the line to add more details. She explained that showing a dog was only one part of the promotion of a top show dog. Advertising his wins in key dog publications was another aspect of the dog game we needed to learn more about. She explained that advertising and promotion costs could equal their handling fees if we were really serious about it.

After clarifying some other points, I rang off and did some deep thinking. "You know, if we are serious about this whole thing, I think we need some good outside advice. Perhaps we should check with Mr. Hallway. He gave us excellent advice when we were getting started," I told Grace.

Grace put in a call to Jim and he agreed to meet with us on Thursday night.

After arriving at Jim's place, we tried to explain our ambition and our confusion about "campaigning" our first dog. Jim nodded his head appreciatively and smiled as we spelled out our dilemma. He had been there before! He had seriously campaigned three Cocker Spaniel Specials to top records.

He described the "smooth" career of the first one, who, like Rudolph, had finished at a very young age and had matured into a top-flight Special. Bomber, a Black-and-Tan, had a rocky start, not placing in the Group under one of Jim's favorite judges. His handler had expressed doubts; if the dog couldn't win under this judge, how could he expect to win under others? "Well," said Jim, "I had some fancy talking to do to convince my handler to stay with the dog. At his second show he placed second in the Group and he was off to the races. In two years he had fourteen Best-in-Show wins, thirty-one Group Firsts, and numerous Group placings. He also won seven Specialty shows. He was retired at three years following his one hundredth Best of Variety win.

"Now, that was the best of all worlds," said Jim. "My second dog, Frosty, was a buff male that finished his championship easily at eighteen months of age. He was to be my handler's number two dog in the Sporting Group. My handler also had good dogs in two other Groups. Well, sir, this was a real complicated problem. My handler didn't have a wife to help him, only young assistants. His number one dog was a nationally ranked Springer Spaniel who nearly always won his breed. There I was, playing second banana to my own handler. A real problem.

"But by putting our heads together we came up with a great solution. We recruited another handler who specialized in Working Dogs but who wanted to break into the Sporting Group to handle Frosty. That worked out great, because Frosty beat the Springer as often as he was beaten. The second year my handler took Frosty full time and he too had an outstanding career.

"The third dog, Bingo, just was a hard luck dog. Not that he wasn't a winner, it's just that he could have done a lot more with a little bit of luck. For example, he would win the breed at a show where the Best-in-Show judge had previously given him a Best in Show and raved about him. If he could have gotten through the Group he could have been a shoo-in for Best in Show. Often as not he would go second or third in the Group and that big win went aglimmering. Let me tell you, campaigning a dog is a tale of 'almosts' and 'could have beens.'

"You see, it's like a baseball game. In baseball you have to get men on base before they can score. In dogs you have to win the breed before you can get into the Group. Getting a Best-in-Show win is tantamount to hitting a grand slam homer. Usually you have to get through three different judges, in the breed, in the Group, and lastly in Best in Show. It's easier said than done.

"Tell me, have I encouraged or discouraged you?"

Grace popped up and said, "Neither, but you do have us intrigued. How would you suggest we start Rudolph?"

Jim thought a minute, and then he said, "If you aren't scared off, then you might make a Specials owner, at that. Before I begin, let me tell you the hardest part of owning a Special. You probably won't make any of the more distant shows, so you will be sitting at home on Saturday and Sunday waiting for the word. Boy, oh boy, you sweat out those phone calls. If the call doesn't come by dinner time you are in anguish because it's so late in the day. Either your dog has gone all the way to Best in Show and your handler is tied up as a result, or your dog bombed and your handler doesn't want to call and give you the bad news. It's enough to give you ulcers. If you notice, the carpet around

the telephone still has the furrows I plowed in it while I was sweating out those calls. I suggest that you have a specific time for your handler to call after each show—win, lose, or draw. While it's more expensive, it's easier on the stomach. Besides, who needs a nervous breakdown to go with the bills?

"Okay, now let's get down to cases. I do have some specific suggestions about Specialing a dog. They are:

"One. Start your dog under the most favorable circumstances. Pick a judge who likes your dog's type and preferably has given him a Best of Breed before.

"Two. Have the dog in *prime* show condition and be sure he is *well* trained.

"Three. In the beginning show *only* under judges who you feel will give you a fair shake and whose reputations you know.

"Four. Remember, the impact of an important win should be felt far beyond the small audience who witnessed the win. *Good* pictures in breed and all-breed magazines *soon* after the win are important.

"Five. Advertise big when you have something to say. Run a constant ad with a 'yearly' look, but change the text, pictures, and size to take advantage of current events.

"Six. In the beginning, stress show wins in your advertising—then bitches being bred to him and then wins of his offspring.

"Seven. Vary pictures of the dog from posed show wins to stop action and informal shots. They must be *excellent* pictures or they come back to haunt you. When in doubt about the quality of a photo, *don't run it.*

"Eight. Even after his show career is off and running, don't enter every show. Some judges are just bad news. Work with your handler to prepare a list of competent judges you will show under.

"Nine. Stress all breed shows and Group winning. Too many dogs are shown only under Specialty judges. Get Rudolph's picture before the all breed judges in an understated but dramatic way. Send a good picture (the judge has to look good too) of all Group and Best in Show wins to each judge, thanking him or her.

"Ten. Be a *good sport*. Take your wins in all modesty. If you lose, congratulate the winner of that day—try to be sincere about it—your turn is next. Build good will for yourself and your dog. This pays off in many ways. Your wins will be popular and people won't use you as the reason for not breeding to or talking up your dog.

"Eleven. *Do not* abuse ring stewards or show officials because you're having a bad day. Be courteous at *all* times.

"Twelve. *Don't gossip! And don't* badmouth your opposition.

"Thirteen. Be sure your dog is treated well in the ring by your handler. Have an understanding that your dog is not be forced if he is having an off day.

"With those guidelines you should be in good shape. You should appreciate the fact that when you decide to Special a dog you enter him in another contest *outside* the show ring. This is for show win points. A number of dog magazines keep track of your dog's winnings and automatically tabulate how he does within his breed, within his Group, and against all comers. Like it or not, he's entered. These magazines usually release their data quarterly. So he's in the running. Once started, it can become an all-consuming passion to have a dog in the top ten winners—I know, I've been there. Be careful you don't sacrifice your integrity and that of your handler just to get those points.

"In addition to these contests, the Quaker Oats Company picks a 'Dog of the Year' and their top choice from each Group to honor at Westminster Show time. Some magazines do the same thing. It gets to be a whole contest within a contest.

"Last, but an extremely important point. *Know when to quit.* Set goals that can be achieved realistically and stay with them. If fifty Best of Breeds within two years is your goal, quit when you get there. There are a number of reasons for this. First, don't wear out your welcome. Believe it or not, people within your own breed will not like your hogging all the top wins. They want a chance too. No matter if yours is the best dog—facts don't count here. Emotions such as envy and jealousy do. To keep good relations in your breed once your dog is out winning, make your realistic goals known. Your fellow competitors can survive since they know there will be an end to your reign.

"I know, I know, you're going to say, 'What if the dog does so fantastically well it would be criminal not to continue to show him? After all he might set records for the breed, etc.' Well, I am sure you will get strong opinions on the other side of this issue, but it is my opinion that if you are going to continue on as a breeder and exhibitor for the long haul, it's better for your strategy to be to 'lose the battle but win the war.' By this I mean that

by giving others a chance you enhance your standing with your neighboring breeders and build your reputation for the long haul. If you become a more senior breeder and have demonstrated that you can breed top dogs regularly, *then* you can really get serious. You will be deserving then. It's just a part of human nature that others will begrudge your wins now but won't ten years from now after you have proven yourself."

Grace and I sat there stunned. "Wow! That's quite a jungle out there, isn't it? All right, what if Rudolph does as well as Marion and Ladislaus think he will? Then what? Are there any returns on our enormous investment?"

"Well, yes and no," said Jim. "There will be trophies galore for top wins. Get yourself a trophy case. Some trophies will be silver or silver plate. Actually, some, such as chafing dishes, bread trays and ice buckets, are usually household items. Of course, with a top winner you start getting lots of duplicates. Additionally, there are many winged-victory type trophies of varying sizes. Money no, trophies yes."

Grace again asked, "Is there any possibility of offsetting our costs?"

"Yes, there is," Jim said, "but not from your show wins themselves. If Rudolph does well, and since he comes from top-flight bloodlines, you could expect a reasonable return from stud services."

"Good, at last a ray of light," I said. "How does that work?"

Jim pointed out that we should get a stud fee somewhere around the low to middle area of what was being asked in our breed, at first. "Then, as his offspring start to win, raise the stud fee to a higher level. Now, before you start counting all that money, you must appreciate the fact that while Rudolph is being campaigned he will be living with his handlers. That means they will be handling the breeding of the bitches sent to your dog, and that you had better find out their terms for picking up bitches at the airport, boarding them until ready to breed, supervising the matings, etc. You may not come out with much in the way of a net profit from each breeding.

"Of course, when he has retired from the show ring and is living at home, you will get all of the stud fee. However, it's now your obligation to pick up the bitches, board them, etc. This means you may want to plan on having a small kennel of your own. You need to look into zoning laws and the like. Don't look so startled. It's all a part of that madness called the 'dog game.'

"If you're still game, and it looks like you are, may I wish you good luck. Please let me know how Rudolph does. If you need any other questions answered, feel free to give me a call."

With Jim's good advice ringing in our ears, we struck out into the night, determined to play the game right the first time around.

Come Blow Your Horn
(How to Advertise What You've Got)

You've heard the old saying, "If you've got it, flaunt it." Well, we were being pushed to do just that. With Rudolph's unprecedented success, we now had the ball in our hands. Would we run, punt, or be tripped up? Frankly, we didn't even know what signals to call.

Obviously, our handlers, Ladislaus and Marion Swiftworthy, wanted to trumpet Rudolph's wins (and their great handling) to the four winds. They pointed out that they had discussed promoting the dog as a part of Specialing him. They also rightfully pointed out that they had told us it probably would cost almost as much to ballyhoo the dog as it did for the handling fees. It was their contention that his wins helped the ballyhoo and the ballyhoo helped the wins. Were they right?

Grace and I sat down to another of our famous powwows. They were called this because "pow," Grace would come up with some spectacular idea, and all I could say was "wow." But on this occasion she had no opening "pow."

For one thing, neither of us knew anything about advertising, although I *had* worked on a couple of advertising campaigns at the office. But was there any similarity? Were dog magazines and newspapers similar to *Playboy, Fortune,* or even the *Reader's Digest?* Who reads dog magazines anyway?

We decided to find out what advertising media were available, the costs, and what kind of audience each drew. Being the shrewd cookies we were, we eliminated network television. Don't laugh! We considered it. When you don't know nuthin', you don't know nuthin'! Seriously, we thought we might be different and investigate TV. However, rational thoughts prevailed. After all, how many owners of Husky bitches could be watching M*A*S*H, then breed to our dog, and enable us to pay back the $50,000 per minute charge? Two million dollars, as simple arithmetic shows (2,000,000 divided by 50,000), will buy forty minutes per year. That's less than one minute per week. If thirty-second commercials were used, eighty commercials could be placed per year—just in case you were wondering why you hadn't seen any stud dog commercials on TV lately.

One major thing we did find out was that there seems to be a great conspiracy participated in by newspapers and magazines (among others) to mislead prospective advertisers about the effectiveness of advertising. Seldom are you told about the many costly campaigns that brought few, if any, stud services, or sold no puppies. Only the positive is accentuated. In fact, Fred Brenning, my company's advertising executive, said, "Companies and individuals would spend less on advertising if they knew the true odds against successful advertising." Fred pointed out that much of advertising's greatest impact is on the advertisers who get a big ego boost out of seeing their ad in print, even though results are negligible.

Since we seemed so interested, Fred sent us down to see Dick Pureheart, the account executive for Roger, Dodger, Foote, Wilson, Hoot & Holler, who handled our company advertising.

Dick would speak only off the record and only if I had nothing to do with my company's advertising. He pointed out that the only reason he would spend some time with us was because he was a dog nut too—Beagles.

Dick started off with a real shocker. He said most advertising fails. When we expressed skepticism about his statement, he said, "If you doubt that most advertising fails, make this test. Pick up yesterday's newspaper. Look through it carefully, page by page, examining each advertisement. Now, how many of the advertisements that were meant to influence you had no effect upon you? Not only did you not read them, you didn't even notice them.

"You can make the test with any large-circulation dog magazine you've already read. Your experience will corroborate known research in this field. On an average, the number of advertisements people pay some attention to during the course of a day is seventy-six. Now, the number they are exposed to is much higher. Seventy-six is simply the number a person paid *some* attention to. With this kind of competition for people's minds, it is impossible for any but comparatively few advertisements to be effective."

Dick went on to say advertising research shows that few people read all the copy in an advertisement. He wondered how many dog advertisers realized that only a small percentage of the readers of any publication in which their advertisement appears will finish reading it. And only a percentage of that group will be favorably influenced, he added. Ouch, I was dreaming of a big double-page spread with a list of every win Rudolph ever made as my big entry splash. Oh well, back to the drawing board.

"Now hold on a minute," said Dick. "I didn't mean to put down advertising in general. But your statement on big size got to me. You know, one of the axioms of advertising is *don't make the advertisement bigger than it need be.* There is evidence, not widely known, that the most economical size advertisement for a newspaper, or a dog magazine for that matter, is one that just dominates the page. A little thought shows why this is so. As the reader turns the page looking for information, his eye is most likely attracted to the largest advertisement on the page. Some readers may look at the other ads, but a good number will not. The dominating advertisement thus gets a bonus in readership. If the advertisement is any bigger than the dominating size, it attracts more readers, but not in proportion to the increase in size. If the advertisement is just less than the dominating size, the drop in readership is likely to be disproportionately great."

On the way home Grace pointed out that we had gotten some good facts from Dick and Fred, but neither talked about advertising in an all breed magazine versus our own breed magazine. "Yeah, and they didn't say anything about trying to appeal to breeders or judges," I added. "Is it possible to do both?"

We slept on it that night, and the next night and the next. In fact I was getting some good sleeping in, as long as I didn't think about the problem. However, all good things come to an end, and Grace came to the dinner table on Friday armed with books, statistics, and pictures. It's a good thing we were only having pot roast. I don't like to have my appetite spoiled like that.

"Look," she said, "I've come up with several conclusions."

"Hold it, hold it," I said. "Before you launch into the stratosphere, where did you glean your facts?"

Smiling like the Cheshire cat, Grace said, "Well, for one, the public library. For another, I went to see Dr. Wendell Householder, you know, the guy we met at the lodge picnic last month. I found out he teaches journalism at the college." Right then I knew the "pow" was coming.

Grace said she had narrowed it down to five major categories. First, how often to advertise; second, how big the ad should be; third, how to avoid common mistakes; fourth, how to get people to do what we want them to do, using words and pictures; and fifth, where to place the advertising to get the best results. Boy, was this gal loaded

for bear! With all her research she probably could give Dr. Householder lessons.

"Okay now, pay attention," she said. "You know how ticked off we get when we see a commercial over and over again on TV? Well, that repetition is good—that's what makes it work. I found out that no matter how good the advertisement is, it won't sell unless it is repeated often, and then you are more likely to remember the brand name and its favorable connotation—so, we've got to push 'Rudolph' and good."

Then I learned that the ratio between size and frequency is not constant. "Huh? Now what's that double talk mean?" I asked.

Grace smiled at me indulgently and explained. "It simply means that, on the average, both readership and responses increase as the size of the advertisement increases. But get this: a full page will not get twice as much attention as a half page. It's common sense that a half-page advertisement will usually be noticed by such a high percentage of readers that it would be impossible to double readership with a full page. On the other hand, a single column ad a couple of inches deep will attract the attention of such a small percentage of readers that doubling its size is likely to double its readership."

"Why didn't you say that in the first place?" I muttered.

"Second, how big? Remember Dick told us something about this. Well, I found out it's true. Dr. Householder said nearly everyone involved with advertising something would like their printed advertisement to be larger than it should be. So both Dick and Dr. Householder agree we shouldn't think 'big' all the time."

"Okay, okay, I can go along with that," I said. "Besides, anything that will keep me out of bankruptcy I support."

Grace gave me a sick smile and went on. "Third, let's avoid common pitfalls."

"Like what?" I asked.

"Like award-winning advertisements are generally

beautiful and entertaining, but the fact is that an ugly advertisement, even an ad that is repulsive to some readers, can be effective." This I had to be convinced of. Grace went on, "Good photographs usually gain more attention than drawings or paintings and are more convincing. Readers accept photographs as objective, as picturing what is real, especially if they are unretouched.

"Now, this book I got out of the library says rectangular photographs gain more attention and are more convincing than other shapes, particularly irregular shapes. So cropped pictures are out. It also says that a single dominant illustration will usually get more attention than multiple illustrations. However, a number of small illustrations scattered throughout the text can increase readership.

"One last zinger on this point. Many advertisements depend on form rather than content because they really don't want to say anything."

"Like a stud dog who hasn't produced or a campaigned Special who is not doing any big winning," I said.

"That's right," Grace said. "Some breeders and exhibitors seem to have so little confidence in what their dog has done or can do that they feel deception is necessary, and yet they really don't want to lie. And, you know, I bet most readers aren't fooled!"

With that last statement I heartily agreed. "You know, Grace, you're on a roll, so why don't you keep on going and I'll save my questions for later."

Thus encouraged, she spread out her material all over the dining room table. Too bad she didn't clear it first. Grease stains are hard to get off of dog photographs.

"My fourth point is to show how to be a proper snake oil salesman," she said.

I couldn't contain myself at that one. "What do you mean by that corker?"

"Well, sir," she said, "you've got to promise and prove to them that you've got a better whatsis than any other guy, like 'get clothes whiter than white.' Or that they'll get something more, like 'get four for the price of three.' You know, aim at their self-interest. The more physical the better: 'a chance to make money,' 'show better taste,' 'have greater sexual attractiveness,' 'have better puppies,' 'put up my dog and be secure that you made the right decision.' That kind of stuff. And you need to back it up with logic. The magic formula is 'to get what you want, do what I want.' For a judge, for example, by citing all the outstanding judges who have put up Rudolph, we get them to identify—'if I do the same I will be right in line with the big guys.' This kind of advertisement doesn't depend upon the head but upon instinct. It aims at the gut, not the brain. This identification advertising can work well because it appeals to the need to belong to a group, and it unifies people."

As I viewed my demure little wife up on her soap box, I feared for our opposition. This gal was intent on wiping them out. No kidding, she meant it.

Relaxing a bit, Grace looked me straight in the eye, and said, "Let's pretend we work for an advertising agency and have to plan a campaign to sell this dog to breeders as a great stud dog, and to judges as a great show dog, for these two nuts who own him."

"Sounds like a good approach," I said. "Let's playact this thing out."

"For starters," said Grace, the professional huckster, "let's address the issue of what media to use. It's apparent that for breeding purposes the big all breed magazines and newspapers probably will not yield the serious breeder business we are looking for. They might tend to reinforce the idea that our dog is successful, so that is some criterion that he has good conformation. But it seems to me that our own breed magazines are the place to talk about pedigrees and his descent from top-producing bloodlines."

As chief copywriter I chimed in to emphasize an area I thought she was missing, namely the kind of campaign we should put on in each type of publication. It didn't matter which one we started with. The early copy could emphasize only his winning and that he came from winning ancestors. "I suggest we start with basically identical ads in one all breed magazine or newspaper that most judges read, and in our own breed magazine.

"In fact, in the breed magazine we might highlight the bitches sent to him as well as his winning ways. Make other people want to get in on the act."

For once Grace sat up and took notice of me. "Ralph," she said, "sometimes you're pretty good when you put your mind to it."

You know, I like my wife, but every once in a while she has to take a cheap shot like that.

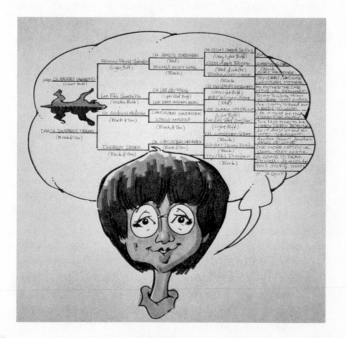

Sportsmanship

"The most important thing in the Olympic games is not to win but to take part, just as the most important thing in life is not the triumph but the struggle. The essential thing is not to have conquered but to have fought well."

    -Baron DeCoubertin
    Founder of the modern Olympic Games

"Winning isn't everything; it's the only thing."

    -Vince Lombardi
    Coach, Green Bay Packers

"When the one Great Scorer comes to write against your name, he marks—not that you have won or lost, but how you played the game."

    -Grantland Rice
    Noted sportswriter

After we had been around the dog show game for a couple of years, Grace and I were continually struck with the incongruity of it all. We went into showing dogs because we were competitive and artistic and wanted to have pride in showing a fine dog.

We have met many fine people as a result of our experiences. On the other hand, we have also encountered some difficult people.

After talking about sportsmanship and ethics a great deal between ourselves, we have come to recognize that the dog show game, like almost all competitive activities, has people involved who cover the complete spectrum of human behavior. People react to wins and losses in entirely different ways. It seems their expectations when entering a show are far different from one another's, as well.

For example, how many times had we heard a group of exhibitors predicting that Ch. Whooziz had this show cold and the rest of us poor suckers didn't stand a chance. Or the tale of Joe Czperwicz, the noted handler of the Outer Mongolian Terrier, who had a show "wired" because the judges had leaned his way in the last show. These and other fairy tales are useful for setting up alibis in advance, so that losses won't seem so bitter. Unfortunately, they also set up a losing attitude and one that fairly screams, "Foul! I only lost because the other guy wasn't playing fair."

Frankly, the way we see it is that in winning and losing,

we have no certainty. Whenever we enter a show, there is a chance we will win. There is also a chance we will lose. As a result, we are always talking in terms of chances or odds.

Are any of these statements familiar to you?

"The odds that a dog will win back-to-back Best in Shows are very high."

"We will probably win the breed today."

"It looks like we may have a seventy percent chance of placing in the Group."

"I feel certain that ninety percent of all judges are honest."

"The odds against your picking a winner from ringside in a large class is probably only slightly better than chance."

Already we have learned that a top class dog should win three out of five times. That's sixty percent. Our handlers have also taught us to "keep a book" on the judges, with detailed records. For example, you will learn in the next chapter that Judge Postwhistle placed Rudolph only third in the Working Group. As it turned out, in talking to him later, he wanted to see more extension in front. This led us to the realization that Rudolph was a bit steep in shoulder, which limited his forward reach. Therefore, we tried to find out which judges put great emphasis on that action and if they might penalize our dog as a result. We did find some who were "front fanatics." As a matter of course, we did not show under them. It's our feeling that we increased Rudolph's winning percentage by five points. It's like a baseball manager looking at his statistics in making out his lineup. If Oscar Crackball has hit a certain lefthander for an average of only .210, he had better use Jeff Strongarm instead, since he has pounded the same guy for a .325 average. If, and it's a big if, winning is everything, then that's the way to go.

Now, by having lived many summers, I have come to realize that winning doesn't come free; it always costs something. For example, by taking this tack I have nagging doubts that my dog can beat all comers under any conditions, and I find it's not always easy to live with that doubt in my mind. Do I have the best, or is it my intent to win only the point races fostered by the dog magazines? Grace and I have rattled that one around aplenty.

Grace says it another way. "If you don't compete, you can't lose—but you can't win either." As I've said before, smart girl, that Grace.

In our rambling discussions with other breeders, both at club meetings and at shows, a number of elements of sportsmanship have come up. For example, this simple truism: in order for there to be a winner, there must be a loser.

Certainly it is apparent that in any breed there can be only a Winners Dog and Bitch, plus a Best of Breed or Variety and Best of Opposite Sex. This leaves many others to ponder why the fates did not choose them. A certain percentage of losers will ascribe their loss to every conceivable reason except the fact that they may have been beaten by a better dog *on that day*.

For some unfortunate people, learning how to lose always eludes them. It is as important as learning how to win. It's the other side of the coin.

Let's be honest—no loser can be termed "happy" by any stretch of the imagination. Turn to the person standing next to you and remark about the poor job of judging and chances are that another soulmate will be found. What's hard about finding another person to agree on that point? However, laud the judge for his discerning ability in placing the best dogs and nine times out of ten you will be greeted by cold stares of incredulousness, dirty looks, nasty remarks, and what have you. For the majority are, by necessity, losers, and the winners are few.

It's hard to be a winner—by any standard. To be a winner is the goal of all and when that goal is reached it often becomes nothing more than a hollow victory. Your dog has won, you're thrilled, elated, on "cloud nine," and you want to shout about it from the rooftops and let the world in on your joy. But you don't—or you have learned not to, because, let's face it, YOU are happy but most of the other exhibitors are not! To have one's dogs' accomplishments greeted by indifference or snide remarks surely takes the wind out of one's sails, and much that should be joyous becomes just the opposite. So, after having come up against the "wet dish rag" treatment, the winner keeps his happiness to himself, and that's not easy. It really is so much easier to mutter under your breath and grumble that you were robbed or that the judge was stupid, because the sympathy of the majority is always with the losers.

Therefore, to be a winner is not easy no matter how desirable the position looks from afar. To come up with winning dogs consistently, year after year, places any breeder in the position of being a prime target for all the unsuccessful, jealous, petty breeders striving for success.

For some reason or another, it seems to be a characteristic of human nature to elevate one's own dogs—not necessarily by *breeding* better dogs, but rather by degrading those belonging to others. Everyone, at one time or another, has been guilty of this to some degree. It might have been due to a slip of the tongue, or in other cases quite deliberately intended. It is usually those on the threshold of success, who perhaps have bred a champion or two, who are the worst offenders. They are striving so desperately to attain their goals that not only do they give little heed to the consideration of others but also they deliberately attempt to undermine the accomplishments of others.

The point should be made that this type of behavior is not confined solely to those engaged in dog activities. It is evidenced even more clearly in the business world by price

cutting, false advertising, and numerous other practices that are frowned on by the Better Business Bureaus.

One requisite necessary for success in dogs is a competitive spirit, and this is something none of the books seems to mention. Obviously, when competitive spirit meets competitive spirit, some sparks are going to fly and there isn't much that can be done to alleviate the situation.

In order for any one breeder to attain success, others must by necessity be hurt along the way. This cannot be helped, for it takes many losers to make a winner. Those on the threshold of success might do well to remember that the time will come, again of necessity, when they must come face to face with some of these same losers on the way back down, for there comes a point in every breeder's endeavors when success can no longer continue to top success, and then there is only one direction in which to go.

Very few, if any, have had the privilege of having their cake and eating it too. That is to say, no one breeder can continually enjoy success, removed from the periphery of the disgruntled. Therefore, the time must come when a choice must be made. Some breeders quit. Perhaps they feel, and rightly so, that they have achieved all that can be achieved and are not content to settle for what would seem to them second best. Others go backwards and gradually fade away, while others learn to compromise. Those who learn to compromise usually end up as the "old timers." Their accomplishments and abilities are recognized, but they no longer hold a monopoly on success. As a result, they hold some popularity amongst their fellows, are no longer the prime target for backbiting, can enjoy their hobby without regarding each new situation as a challenge, and no longer need continually to prove their dogs' values in the scheme of things. The aspiring breeder is striving always and it is this very aggressiveness which helps achieve success, but, at the same time, which calls undesirable instincts into play.

It is all very well and good for one to say that because his or her dogs are the object of nasty remarks, it proves that they are good dogs. In fact, some people have been known to say they welcome the backbiting and innuendos because to them it is proof of their dog's worth. People may say this, but deep down they really can't mean it, for any situation of this type is uncomfortable and not easy to live with. The desire for recognition is one thing, but there also is a desire for acceptance. As a result, successful breeders are usually very lonesome people. For to be up on top in any locale is to be pretty much alone. There just isn't room at the top for many. This cannot be recognized by those aspiring for success. This can be truly understood only by those who have experienced the success, with its accompanying drawbacks. For whereas the attainments differ from individual to individual, the resulting experiences are usually the same.

To be a good winner takes a very thick skin. When the nasty remarks and innuendos begin to filter through, it is almost humanly impossible to resist them. Most breeders fight back in one way or another for a while. The ways in which a breeder can fight back are many—he can fight back vocally, or in the show ring, or through the printed word. Perhaps there is a measure of satisfaction to be gained by attempted retaliation, but usually little or nothing is accomplished other than intensifying an already painful situation. It should not be implied that the only solution would be to fold one's tent and quietly sneak away. As stated previously, it takes only a thick skin! Just ask any breeder.

If one will but note, the people who show the point makers, the losers, are always *nice* people, and their dogs are really not too bad. Perhaps they are shown improperly or groomed improperly but other than that receive little or no "lip service." But that *other* fellow, you know, the one who is consistently taking the points or the Variety or the Group, well, he wouldn't sell *you* a good dog, now would he? And *how* he can continually win with *that* stuff he

shows! The judge must be blind or else a personal friend! All this should sound familiar.

I remember one show where I saw a perfect example of learning to lose with grace. Jim and Tammy had a hot winning Saluki. In fact, he had dominated the breed and Group for the first five months of the year. Then, at their big Specialty, an Australian judge of some repute chose another dog for BOB. This dog had been playing second fiddle all year.

At the club banquet that night the owners of the Best of Breed dog were virtually ignored and were very depressed. Just when they should have been enjoying one of the high points of their dog life they were being put down. The evening turned around when Tammy called the group to attention and offered a toast to the dog and his owners for the great win. That broke the ice and the rest of the evening went well for all.

It was a perfect example of how it is possible to win and lose at the same time. Turning it around the other way, Jim and Tammy, because of that sporting gesture, became winners in everyone's minds, including the owners of the dog that defeated theirs. Too many people believe that only winning is positive and that losing is always negative. Actions such as Tammy's prove it doesn't have to be so.

Another reflection on this winning thing involves the time Judge Postwhistle placed Rudolph third in the Group. Our sights had been set on winning the Group and then shooting for Best in Show. The BIS judge had put us up before and we figured we had a fighting chance to go all the way. We were really downcast after the Group. Then along came this young couple who were even greener in the dog game than we were and offered effusive congratulations on Rudolph's wonderful win. I guess it's a matter of perspective. What may seem like a loss to one person may seem like a win to someone else.

In the first years of our marriage Grace and I weathered some real storms, and that taught us always to look on the brighter side of things. We learned quickly that showing dogs was only one facet of our lives. Winning was exhilarating, losing was not. However, we had each other, our work, our nice home, and now our dog hobby. Put into perspective, our hobby is fun, but it will not dominate our lives totally. As in dog construction, balance is important to a well-rounded life. We felt sorry for those people who must try to achieve all their satisfaction in the dog world because they get so little in the "outside" world.

We have also become much more sympathetic toward the judges' dilemma. After all, it's rarely possible to please everyone. All we can ask is a conscientious job and a knowledge of our Standard. And by and large, we see this happen, week after week. It's amazing how many dedicated and knowledgeable people are in the judge's ranks. We have learned to sit back and appreciate their skills. We sure wish more people would.

Learning the Fundamentals of Gait

After being around the dog game for a while, I thought I had begun to know a little something about conformation. There was one problem, however: I really couldn't tell if a dog was a good mover or not. Oh sure, I could tell if he was sidewinding, or if he was high in the rear, and even if he moved close behind. But I really didn't know why a dog did those things. Going over a posed dog really gives you only part of the picture, I was told.

A short time before, we had shown Rudolph under Judge Wilmont Postwhistle at the Monumental Hills show. Rudolph placed third in the Group that day and the judge remarked to our handler that he would like to see more extension in the front. We had always thought Rudolph was pretty good there, so we were a bit confused. As we talked to Judge Postwhistle afterwards, I guess he saw that we really wanted to learn more about gait. He invited us up to his place, which was about forty miles up the road, one night the following week to talk about the fundamentals of gait.

When we arrived he had a slide projector all set up. He said he was going to teach us the ABC's of motion and then we could talk further. Off went the lights and the first slide came up.

"Many an old-time breeder considered movement to be the 'proof of the pudding.' Such statements as 'a dog ain't worth nothin' if he can't go in the field,' and 'a dog that can't put meat on the table shouldn't be kept,' were often made. So the old-timers reasoned, and they were correct. They were talking about a sound dog," said Judge Postwhistle.

"Soundness should mean that the animal is able to carry out the job for which it is intended, as in this slide of a Retriever bringing in a duck. It should mean that he is free from flaw, healthy, and capable of lasting endurance. The basic purpose of breeding purebred dogs for the show and field is to produce specimens which can approach this ideal."

He said, "I am going to discuss some basic facts about movement, which may upset some of your preconceived ideas about how an animal moves. Most importantly, I want you to understand how a properly built dog *should* move and to recognize that deviations from proper movement are caused by incorrect construction.

"Gait is a small word but a very complex subject, so it is best to start with something that is easily understood. A proper definition of two terms appears to be of the utmost importance. The first is equilibrium, which means all forces in balance, and the second is stability, which means maintaining equilibrium to keep all forces in balance.

"Now, Ralph, I want you and your lovely wife to know that discriminate breeding over the years has produced many fine breeds, each developed for a particular purpose. With the exception of perhaps a few Toy breeds, all dogs of any merit have one trait in common with each other—the ability to do their jobs with the least amount of effort.

"Before we tackle how the dog actually moves, let's take a look at what makes it move. Scientists have defined two sorts of actions: those involving recognized preliminaries, or voluntary actions, and those which require no thinking to get them done, or involuntary actions. The latter, which are governed by a bodily system called the autonomic nervous system, gets its actions done by 'just doing it.'

"Of course, it can be shown that these actions are preceded by all sorts of physiological events—the contraction of muscles, the stimulation of nerves—but when a dog moves his foot, he doesn't choose to move his muscles first and then find to his delight that his foot has moved. What he does is simply move his foot.

"Let's take a minute to try to find out why and how it happens so we can better understand what is behind the action of a dog as we observe it moving.

"When a nerve stimulates a muscle, the result is very similar to what happens when the firing pin of a gun detonates a charge of gunpowder. The force with which a bullet is discharged from the pistol is much greater than the force with which the firing pin strikes. The movement of the bullet is caused by the explosive charge and *not* by the mechanical impact of the hammer: as long as the impact is forceful enough to detonate the gunpowder, the gun will go off, and the power of the explosion is entirely proportional to the amount of explosive in the cartridge. It is an *all* or *nothing* affair. As I said, this is similar to what happens when a muscle goes off. An explosive charge of chemical energy is stored in the muscle, and as long as this is triggered by a nerve stimulus of the right size, it will always release the same amount of energy.

"Now, the only way to increase the power of a muscle is to multiply the number of muscle fibers involved. This is similar to pulling two triggers simultaneously on a double-barreled shotgun.

it is a question of *frequency*: the stronger the stimulus, the more impulses dispatched down the nerve, so that the intensity is defined by the *number* of impulses, rather than by the size of any one of them. It's like a series of flames coming upon the heels of each other as they go down the gunpowder trail. Got that?

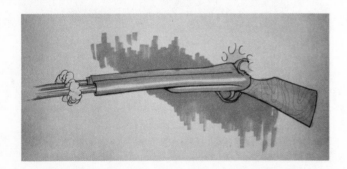

"Unfortunately, the gun analogy breaks down at this point because the nerve really supplies no mechanical impact to the muscle. The nerve doesn't move. It doesn't strike the muscle but acts like a trail of gunpowder with the impulse traveling along it like a flame. When it arrives at the muscle, the muscle blows up like a keg of gunpowder.

"Grace, you're wiggling in your seat something fierce so you must have seen the flaw in this analogy immediately. What you want to ask is this: if the size of the nerve impulse is always the same, regardless of the stimulus that provokes it, how in the world does the dog go faster— right? Never fear, modern science has an answer! You see,

"Okay, now we are ready to talk about movement itself. It is important to understand that a prerequisite to good movement is balance between the front and the rear assemblies. The dog should be able to balance his forequarter action with the propulsion supplied by the rear quarters so that he can reach forward without constriction in a full stride, maintaining his equilibrium, and moving on as straight a line as possible. Above all, his gait should be coordinated, smooth, and effortless. The dog must cover ground with his action, and excessive animation should never be mistaken for proper gait. One needs to understand that movement, or action, is the crucial test of conformation. At present there is a great deal of speculation as to whether the front or rear limbs provide the major propulsive power, and at what speeds, and at what intervals. It is, most likely, a shared responsibility.

31

"You, Ralph, and Grace too, I am sure you have discovered it is not easy to explain movement with words, but if you will visualize yourself standing in the middle of a railroad track with a locomotive engine coming toward you, then replace the engine with a dog, you will get a pretty accurate idea of correct fore and aft gait. It will be apparent that when a dog is coming to you at a trot, nothing should be visible but head, chest, and front legs. The legs should reach forward at every stride, perfectly straight from the shoulders, with feet absolutely parallel to the legs, as though traveling on a single track. If you get glimpses of its hind feet, side, rump, and tail, it's sidewinding or rolling, both due to structural faults.

"As the train moves away from you, nothing should be visible but the caboose. Now substitute a dog and we

should see only the back of the dog's head, the top of his back to the buttocks, and his hind feet, with the legs traveling parallel at each stride. The same principles of locomotion apply as in front movement.

"To truly understand a breed, it is necessary to understand why the breed was bred to move as it does. To do so, one needs to know the purpose for which the dog was bred. As contrasted with the Terriers, which employ their front feet for digging, and the Hounds, many of which are not required to have excessive speed, the Sporting breeds use their front legs like a rudder on a ship, for navigational purposes.

"I don't know if you are aware of it or not but there are many different means of locomotion. The three most common in the show ring are the walk, the trot, and the pace. To give a clearer understanding, I will discuss and describe the walk and the trot. I would like to emphasize in the beginning that the trot is the basic gait and that the pace is incorrect.

"Let's lead off with the premise that in any type of movement, body support, to be efficient, must be under the center of gravity of the body. Visualize, then, an imaginary line drawn through the center of the dog's body from the tip of the nose to the end of the tail. It will be on this line that action will take place.

"This may sound illogical because we all know that in most breeds the dog's legs are very nearly perpendicular to the ground when the dog is at rest. When the dog starts a slow walk, its legs remain pretty much in the same position. Because the eye can follow a slow walk, but cannot follow fast movement, you probably thought that perpendicular leg action applies to all gaits. But in trotting dogs, this is not possible when the body is supported by only one or two legs. Aside from the change in speed, the basic difference between the walk and the trot is that at the walk the dog's body is supported at three points, while at the trot it is supported at two. In the walk the center of gravity is always within the triangle created by three limbs placed stably on the ground. Therefore, the animal can stop moving at any time and still not fall to the ground.

"Because it is the walk that we can see with the naked eye, it is easy to see why it is assumed that this is the natural gait of the dog when moving. Based upon this popular misconception, structural faults, which in a true gait are easily discernible, are never truly identified by some because of their lack of awareness of the components of proper gait, which *do not* come into play in the walk.

"You have to realize that the walk is a gait of convenience, not of efficiency. Now, take an airplane racing down a runway with its nose wheel down. This method is employed to gather speed until its nose wheel lifts off the ground, and then the plane is in its true flight attitude. So it is with most dogs as they gather speed and shift to their truly efficient gait, the trot.

"If you look closely and know what you're looking for, you can see that in a trot, each foot is lifted *before* its predecessor in the cycle has touched the ground, and thus the left front foot moves forward with the right rear so that balance is maintained on one point on each side. As the dog follows through, the opposing two legs, right front and left rear, take over to propel it forward. A pattern of 'convergence toward a center line' takes over at this point, which means moving forward on one line of progress with the least muscular waste. This is often called 'single tracking.' In this sequence of events there is a brief period when the animal is supported by only two of its four limbs. This makes for greater momentum but less stability. This movement is in contrast to 'double tracking' with the perpendicular leg action of the slow walk. Any questions?"

"Yes," I said. "If the dog is being supported by two legs, how does he maintain his balance and not stagger around the ring?"

"Good question," said old Judge Postwhistle. "The dog can be likened to a rectangular table, supported on each of its four corners by wooden legs. In the dog these legs are replaced by flexing limbs that seldom provide a perfectly smooth ride for the middle piece. This happens because the under support is never exactly equal, and some up-and-down or vertical movement is to be expected and probably can be considered desirable. Further, some torsion or twisting motion is to be expected, although in the ring we want our dogs to move forward in a level fashion as viewed from the side. We also want them to move forward in a straight line as viewed from the rear. As a by-product of this type of movement we see a rolling effect, causing the dog to move from side to side as he travels forward. I'm sure that both of you have seen this many times in the ring. Technically, this is known as lateral displacement.

"As we have seen, the dog is seldom supported continuously by all four limbs as he moves. In the simple trot cycle, he is supported by only two. These alternate corner supports are like a table with only two legs, their location being at diagonal corners. As a result, a lack of

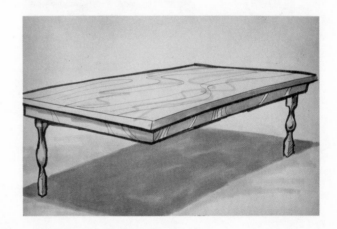

stability can easily occur. To partially compensate for these lateral displacement stresses, the dog will often shift his moving limbs inward to produce the so-called single tracking tendency. If this does not take place, such as in the excessively wide-fronted dogs, a rolling or twisting action is apt to be most noticeable in the rear quarters. In Terriers it's different, where there is a pendulum-like trot that has the forelegs swinging parallel with the sides, with a minimum of convergence.

"As I pointed out, a properly moving dog is one that moves with his feet converging toward a center line. As you can see in the ring, when the dog is moving away there will be a straight line of bone from the hip to the pad. A close-moving dog will have a break in this line of bone. Remember, when a dog moves at a trot his feet should seek out the center of gravity. This means that his feet will be hitting *under* the center line of his body. Therefore, his legs *will not* be perpendicular to the ground. If they are, he is moving under the corners. A dog that moves in this manner is forced to work harder than a dog which moves properly.

"Now, Grace, if you will pay close attention and not daydream about all the Best-in-Show wins that Rudolph will attain, I will attempt to explain the criteria judges use to determine whether or not a dog is an efficient mover. It's simply the dog's ability to move in a straight, level line. An example might make this a little clearer. Ralph, if you were to walk four or five blocks, the chances are that you would not be too tired when you finished, right? However, if you hopped the same distance, you probably would be

quite exhausted. Why? Because you propelled yourself much higher than was necessary to travel the distance forward. Your center of gravity was being moved forward in an unnecessarily high arc—from the ground to the peak of the hop and back to the ground. Energy was being spent to move you up when all you wanted to do was go forward.

You would also be tired because your legs received an extra jolt from the hard landing after each hop.

"Now that you have assimilated that, here is another new fact for you. Did you know that all the muscles in the dog are in a mild state of contraction even when there is no observable movement? It's true. Even Rex sleeping over

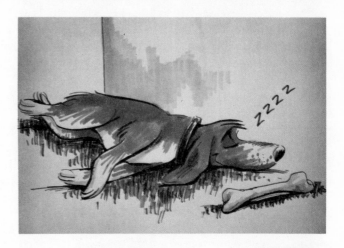

there in the corner qualifies. In fact, the maintenance of a static position such as this is just as active and just as strenuous as the movements that arise from it. In order for old Rex to stand, for instance, the muscles which oppose one another on either side of his patella, hip, and hock, must exert an equal and opposite tension. This stabilizes the joints and prevents them from folding up under the animal's weight.

"Now, listen carefully, because this is important stuff. Strictly speaking, movements are simply modifications of posture, which take the dog from one stable stance to the next: the dog re-sculpts itself from moment to moment. When he moves one of his limbs, it increases the state of contraction on one side of the joint and subtracts or extinguishes a proportional amount on the other.

"Let me get organized here. It's probably a good idea to start at the front of the dog and work back, so let's talk about the importance of the head and neck in the total movement picture. Did you know that many Standards contain words like 'neck—moderately long, and smoothly fitting into the shoulders'? It is very essential for you to understand exactly what functions the head and neck carry out in regard to movement. Believe it or not, when the dog stretches out his neck, the weight of his neck and head upsets his balance. That's true! This causes the dog to literally have to catch up with himself. This neck extension lets gravity pull at the head and neck. Now, if the handler holds the dog's head too high, there would be no upsetting of balance and the dog would have to work harder to move. Many a dog that is forced to move with his head too high has to work *too* hard. This is wasted energy, and improper movement results. No dog should drag his head on the ground, but he must be given the opportunity to upset his balance. Watch your dog in the yard; generally, the head is up but it is not held high. If you view the dog in profile, you can imagine a clock with the center of the shoulders as the center of the clock. Then, the head and shoulders, depending upon the breed, are anywhere from 9:30 to 12:30 on the clock. This table illustrates characteristic head carriage for a variety of breeds.

Typical Head Carriage
(Dog Moving at Trot)

Breed	Elevation
Irish Setter	9:30-10:30
Cocker	9:00-9:30
Collie	10:00
Chow	9:00-9:30
Beagle	9:30-9:45

"When a dog starts to move he lifts the shoulders first and swings them forward. He raises and contracts the neck muscles to do it. The muscles that we are talking about attach to the wings of the vertebrae. A dog that is built for strength has short, thick muscles in the neck and shoulders. A dog that is built for movement and speed has long and slender muscles in the neck, such as those of a gazehound. A longer neck permits longer muscles, thereby contributing to better movement because longer muscles tire less easily.

"Another reason for a long neck is to aid in locomotion by helping to shift the center of gravity or balance point of the dog. A longer one has much more effect than does a shorter one—a simple principle of leverage.

"A dog must 'have its head' in gaiting so that he can use his neck for proper lift of his upper arm. A tight lead yields head movement, not neck movement.

"Tell me, how many times have you seen a good dog going along on a really tight lead and acting like a spastic alligator? Head high, good, but legs going every which way. It looks all wrong.

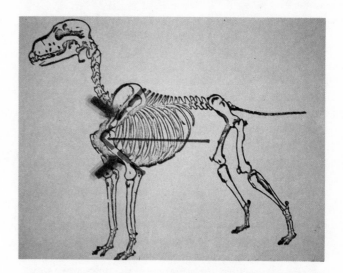

"Now, let's continue with the forequarters. In the 'ideal' front assembly the shoulder angle enables the third and fourth ribs, the largest and deepest ones, to reach the elbow, but not to reach to such a depth as to interfere with easy and free movement of the upper foreleg. This assembly should produce shoulders that are fine at the points and clearly cut at the withers. 'Fine at the points' refers to the point where the shoulder blades meet the upper arms and control the width of the front section, when viewed from the front. 'Clearly cut at the withers' refers to the distance between the shoulder blades when felt at the top of the withers. The shoulder blade should be closely set with little distance between blades.

"Placement of shoulder and the angle between it and the upper arm create the major deviations in the front end assembly. Straight shoulders have plagued many breeds. There is reason for this. In order to put the dog up on his legs and give him a more 'forward' look, the bones were spread, through selective breeding for a number of generations, and this resulted in rotating the shoulder forward both at the withers and at the elbow. As a result, it is easier to produce a 'Terrier-fronted' specimen in a racy type of dog. Many such specimens, although elegant in outline, appear 'leggy' and lack depth of brisket. In this

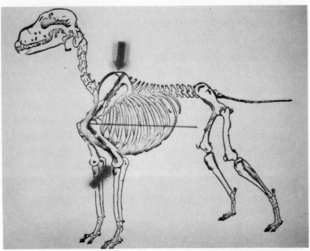

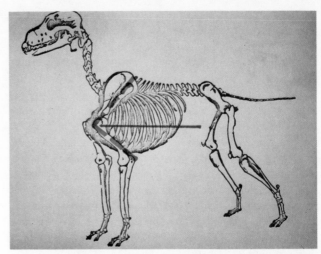

type of assembly, the chest, in most cases, would be set further back than the points of the shoulders, presenting a shallow-chested effect. Movement, of course, would be more stilted, with a minimum of reach, resulting in a choppy action which covers little ground.

"It should be noted that not all breeds should have long and sloping shoulders. Some should have slightly sloping ones instead. Such shoulders are found on dogs where speed and sudden movements are not commonplace. Some breeds need power more than speed. As a result, their Standards may call for moderately sloping shoulders. They are usually accompanied by a comparatively straighter rear.

"Next, let us turn our attention to the dog's front shock absorbers, the pasterns. We have learned through experience that a shoulder blade which is long and slopes toward a thirty-four to thirty-nine degree angle in perspective with the ground, allows the pastern to provide the maximum shock-cushioning during the stride. The pasterns are more important to the soundness of the dog than most people realize. The pasterns act like shock absorbers on a motorcycle. Proper pasterns cushion the impact of each step, thereby reducing the shock received by the shoulders. Good pasterns, as far as most breeds are

concerned, are not straight, but rather should have a slight but definite angle to them in relation to the bones of the forearm. This angle supplies a certain amount of 'give' as a result, and gradually diminishes the shock of each step. Straight pasterns have little 'give' and must pass the impact directly to the shoulder. There should be just enough bend at the joint to indicate visually a difference in the line of the bone. It should be noted that some Terrier Standards call for pastern joints that have little bend.

"In those breeds calling for a well-laid-back shoulder, the Standard usually states that the upper foreleg of the dog should be as long as the shoulder blade, and should form a ninety degree angle with the shoulder blade. However, recent research has indicated that a shoulder blade angle of thirty-four to thirty-nine degrees is what is found on most winning dogs, while the upper arm angle of forty-five degrees does not seem challenged. Thus, an angle of seventy-nine to eighty-four degrees is reasonable. This combination seems to allow for the maximum amount of ground to be covered per stride. It is apparent that any other combination will force the dog to work harder to cover the same area.

"Some writers feel the front is relatively more important than the hindquarters. While this may be

debatable, there are certain points in its favor. This can be demonstrated. If, for example, you were to take an Irish Setter and place his front feet on one scale and his rear feet on another, you would find that about sixty percent of the weight of the breed is carried by the forequarters. The longer the dog's neck and head, and the more elegant his carriage, the further forward is the center of gravity and the greater the proportion of weight on the forequarters. So, by merely supporting the mass, you might say the front works fifty percent harder than the rear, even before a step is taken.

"The shoulder blade itself is attached to the rib cage by means of muscles both on top of and underneath the blade. These muscles, as do all muscles, act in pairs. We have learned that when one expands, the other contracts. They also are alike in size. If the outer muscles are heavy and coarse, the ones underneath will also be heavy and coarse. Because of this, a mass of muscles at the shoulder will cause the blade to be pushed too far away from the rib cage and give the dog what is called 'loaded shoulders.' This in turn leads to a dog's being out at the elbows.

"Why is it so important for a dog not to be 'out at the elbows'? The best way to explain it is simply to say that a straight column of bones can support weight more easily than a bent column can. Another disadvantage to the loaded shoulders is that such conformation makes it almost impossible for the dog to jump properly, for on the way down the dog almost always lands on his face. Many dogs with loaded shoulders will refuse to jump because they have learned the consequences.

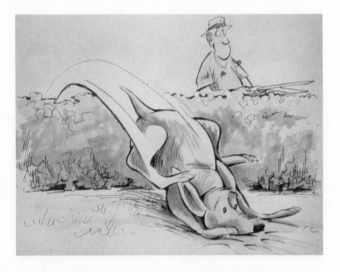

"Okay, so far we have learned that the hardest working part of the dog is the front. It has more functions to perform than any other assembly, and takes more of a beating. It supports the major part of the weight of the dog, acts as a shock absorber, and is the first part of the dog to the food bowl.

"The next area for study is the body. Most Standards describe the ideal body as sufficiently long to permit a straight and free stride. They call for deep chests, reaching approximately to the elbows, with adequate width in front, and ribs that are well sprung. The length of body is important to good movement. No matter how well the legs, shoulders, hips, and other parts, are assembled, if the body is too short the rear legs will interfere with the front. Well-sprung ribs are also a key to movement. If the elbows are close to the body, a barrel-shaped body will force the elbows out. Conversely, a shelly, thin body allows the elbows to be too close. Both hamper efficient movement.

"Generally speaking, the middle piece should be short. The length of the dog should be in the forehand and rearhand. Many Standards also call for a short, level back—within reason of course.

"Let's clear up some confusion as to where the back is located. The general concensus is that it starts at the withers and extends to the base of the tail. In reality, this is the top line. The back is a very short section of the top line that starts approximately at the last ribs, reaching forward for about five additional ribs.

"It is important to note that all dogs have a slight rise to the loin. The vertebrae get thicker from the back to the pelvis because it is here that the lumbar vertebrae lock together to form a double articulation, giving greater strength.

"The great majority of breed Standards call for or suggest the desirability of such an arched loin by using such terms as 'strong,' 'muscular,' 'moderate length,' 'powerful and wide,' in their written descriptions.

"It is now time for us to discuss the hindquarters. Many Standards state something like the following about the hindquarters: 'wide and powerful, with broad, well-developed thighs, hind legs long and muscular from hip to hock, short and nearly perpendicular from hock to ground; well angulated at the stifle and hock joints, which like the elbows, incline neither in nor out.'

"The hindquarters are not designed to support weight, but to push off. Because of this, the hindquarters must be muscular and strong, with proper angulation. A correct hindquarter assembly will provide maximum drive, lift, and power for propulsion. We have learned that the force of gravity is responsible when the head and neck upset balance, but because gravity causes the parts to descend at the same rate of speed, the dog is quite literally pushed forward by its hind legs while falling. The propulsive power is then transmitted and shared with the front legs.

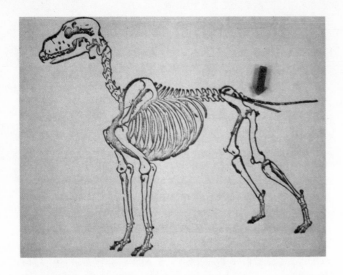

"The reasons for wanting a thirty degree angle to the set of the croup or pelvis are twofold. First, a thirty degree angle permits the rear leg to swing backward much more than does a steep croup. Understanding that a major portion of the dog's power is derived from the leg during its backward swing should help you realize why we want a long backstroke. The second reason is that a flat croup permits longer muscles from it to the stifle. These are also part of the group of muscles that draw the leg back and also part of the group of muscles that add power to the drive. As you will recall, one of the functions of the front was to try to maintain a level center of gravity by keeping the front in balance, or stable. It will check the potential fall arising from each step. Remember, the purpose of the hindquarters is just the opposite. It upsets the center of gravity by helping to propel it forward. As we have learned, movement is the shifting of this balance point. It is the balance that exists between the front of the dog and its rear that makes it a good or bad animal from the standpoint of movement. A dog having a front that is capable of handling a thrust of fifty pounds is out of balance if the rear delivers a thrust of one hundred pounds. It is far better to have them both at fifty pounds.

"The pelvis, or croup area, that portion of the spinal column from the last vertebra of the loin to the first vertebra of the tail, should be at a thirty degree slope in

relation to the dog's back. The upper leg and femur should intersect the slope of the pelvis at a ninety degree angle. Running an imaginary line through the hock, perpendicular to the ground, the upper and lower thigh bones connect in such a way as to form a forty-five to fifty degree angle. Remember, a dog with these angles gets a maximum drive extension out of the rear legs with the hindquarters being the propelling force continually upsetting balance, and forcing the front to either catch the body or fall. Both the femur and the thigh bone should be approximately the same length as the shoulder blade, balancing the dog front to rear.

"You will recall that we touched on the fact that in Standards that do not call for a forty-five degree shoulder angle it is usually stipulated that the rear legs must be moderately angulated. This is in sharp contrast to the extreme rear angulation found on many breeds where the Standard calls for the forty-five degree shoulder. The moderate rear does not propel the dog beyond its shoulders, and most importantly it provides more direct useable power. Evidence exists that the most efficient way to transfer power from the rear to the animal itself is in a straight line. Therefore, the leg with little angulation presents a more compact, straighter line, than does a well-angulated leg.

"Now, Ralph and Grace, pay particular attention, for I want to sum it all up. As I pointed out to you, a properly moving dog is a thing of beauty. Both front and rear legs should reach full extension. To achieve this, the front foot should be snatched out of the way a split second before the rear foot comes down in literally the same spot.

"I hope the two of you now have a better appreciation of Rudolph's strong and weak points, for I have attempted to show the links between characteristics of gait and conformation, and to ascribe faulty gait to faulty body construction. However, as you have learned through showing, it is not structure alone that makes a winner. Condition, attitude, and TLC, all contribute to the dog's performance. Therefore, show dogs must be judged 'on the day.'

"A final word regarding balance in action seems appropriate. Oftentimes one hears the expression 'all of a piece,' which really sums it all up, in that the dog described is well balanced both in stance and in action."

"The most obvious faults to be considered when viewing the hindquarters from behind are cow hocks and open hocks. Generally, specimens that have cow hocks are dogs with *heavier* quarters and *straight* stifles. The specimens with open hocks generally have adequate angulation but a slighter musculature.

"It is, I think, often not appreciated that dogs which step out strongly and show marked drive with the hind legs, are almost always longer in thighs, from hip to hock, than those which step short and lack drive in the hind action. The extra length in the upper and second thigh bones is directed forward, thus giving a marked curve along the front of the hind leg, known familiarly as the bend of stifle.

"Along with wanting a dog to have adequate speed, we also want endurance; and this endurance or staying power is determined by the relationship of the hock and the lower thigh. Many Standards call for 'hocks well let down.' This statement translates into endurance. A well-let-down hock means that the hock should be relatively short when compared to the lower thigh bones. As the hock lengthens, the lower thigh bones shorten, increasing speed but decreasing staying power. The rear leg of a rabbit is extremely long. Therefore, the rabbit is very fast for a short distance. While the rabbit can initially outrun a Beagle, the Beagle invariably will catch up after a few minutes' run.

Applying Science to Dog Breeding

Taking the advice Jim Hallway had given us when we first considered campaigning Rudolph, we had a long and interesting meeting with our handlers, and we thrashed out all the details of Rudolph's Specials career. Luckily they were in almost complete agreement with what Jim had to say, but they offered one other suggestion which we acted on.

They pointed out that it would take a while before other breeders really took note of Rudolph and bred their bitches to him. By that time his show career could be coming to an end and there would be no winning puppies to keep him in the public eye. They suggested we seriously study genetics and then buy two good bitches to breed to him, and get his offspring out to the matches and shows. After all, they said, if you don't breed to him, others will wonder.

Taking this sage advice, we purchased *The Standard Book of Dog Breeding*, published by Denlinger's Publishers, Ltd., and this is what we learned:

The consistent breeding of show quality specimens depends on other important factors besides the natural or acquired talents of the breeder. Many breeders still operate under the illusion that second best will produce as well as the choice specimen, pedigrees being equal. This will hold true in isolated instances, of course, but it will not hold true consistently.

Another most important element contributing to the success or failure of any given breeding program is that of chance or luck. Everything else being equal, sex distribution, puppy mortality, timing, transmission of the best factors, or the poorest, etc., all depend to a great extent on chance or luck.

It was apparent from our show experience and from our reading that the first step in any animal breeding program is to decide what is ideal. Until we understood what kind of specimen we wanted, we would be stopped cold and could neither select the best nor discard the worst. This is where our breeder's capabilities came into play, for this is the basis of selective breeding, which serves as the backbone of any successful breeding program.

One of the next things we learned is that characteristics such as height and coat color are known as "inherited" traits. They are traits which an offspring "inherits" or receives from his parents. Every living thing has an inheritance, or heredity. Inherited traits are passed along from generation to generation. As a result of heredity, each generation is linked to past generations. A Doberman may resemble his parents with respect to height and the Red/Tan pattern. His grandsire or great grandsire also may have possessed the same identifying features.

A whole science known as genetics has grown up around the study of heredity. Specifically, the science of genetics is the study of how the reproduction process determines the characteristics of an offspring and of how these characteristics are distributed.

Gregor Mendel, a nineteenth-century monk living in Czechoslovakia, is credited as the founder of the science of genetics. Basically, Mendel's work proved that traits can be passed from one generation to the next, with mathematical precision. Before his time, it had been assumed that inheritance was always a matter of blending, as if colored water was added to plain water, with the result being colored water of a weaker hue. Mendel proved that genes, the differing units of inheritance, are distinct entities. They do not blend, like colored water. They can produce, to continue the analogy, plain water, colored water, or a mixture between the two. Moreover, assuming no other genes are involved to complicate the story, they continue to create these three kinds of products in generation after generation.

The mathematics has a pleasing simplicity, at least in the early stages. The human blue-eye/brown-eye situation is a good and elementary example. There are genes for brown and genes for blue, and as a simple example we may say that everybody receives one of each from each parent. To receive two browns is to be brown-eyed. To receive two blues is to be blue-eyed. To receive one of each is also to be brown-eyed because the brown has the effect of masking the relative transparency of the blue.

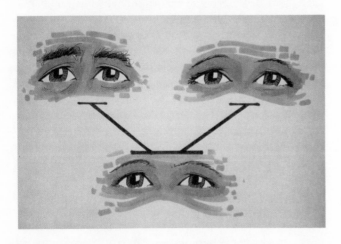

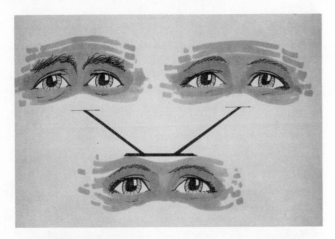

At first it was assumed that all inheritance was equally clear-cut, with the ratio of three to one, or Mendel's famous ratio of nine to three to three to one (involving two characteristics), explaining all of our genetical fortunes. This is true, in a sense, but the real situation is much more complex. Only a few aspects of inheritance are controlled by a single pair of genes. Only a few more are controlled by two pairs. A feature such as height, for example, or coat color, may be organized by twenty or so pairs. Each pair is working in a Mendelian manner, but the effect of them all working together is a bewilderment. The mathematics still have the same precision, but are explanatory only for mathematicians, not for the rest of us. As for a feature like intelligence, with the brain differentiated to fill the tremendous range of different tasks, its inheritance cannot be thought of in a simple ratio of any kind.

There are literally thousands and thousands of paired genes within each animal. There are enough of them, and enough possible variations, to ensure that each specimen is unique. For example, we learned that never before in history had there been a single specimen just like Rudolph, and that never in all of future history will there be one exactly like him again. It was amazing to find out

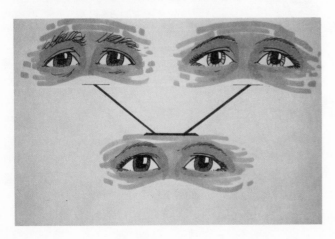

that he is a combination that is entirely individual, and yet his genes are common to the entire population of Siberian Huskys. There is nothing unique about them, and even their offspring, because of sexual reproduction, can spring from Rudolph's loins with only fifty percent of what he could give them.

I want to pause here and see if I can describe what a gene is. We found out that we are unlikely ever to see a gene but we surely can see its remarkable effects.

Scientists, using electron microscopes, have measured the length of a gene from 0.0034 millimeters up to twice that size. In width it is only 0.002 microns (a micron is one-thousandth of a millimeter).

The gene is composed of an acid with a tongue twister name, deoxyribonucleic acid, commonly called DNA. The name of the acid comes from a sugar that it contains. Biologists now believe that a molecule of DNA consists of two long chains, nucleotides, that coil slightly to form a double helix (a double spiral).

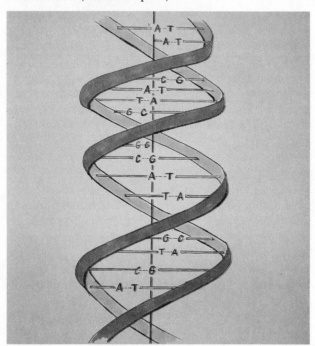

Genes are arranged within chromosomes. Dog body cells contain thirty-nine pairs of chromosomes, or a total of seventy-eight.

The center of a cell is called a nucleus. The instructions for most of the cell's activities come from small structures in the nucleus, the chromosomes.

When a cell reaches a certain size, it may divide into two cells. Before this happens, one chromosome moves to one side of the cell, while its duplicate moves to the other side. The two cells then have exactly the same kind and number of chromosomes as the original cell. In animal reproduction, female and male sex cells come together to start this interaction.

Now I want to piggyback upon the work of Mendel and later scientists and see how we can take their knowledge and become better breeders.

We now know that each dog has in each of its cells, a pair of genes for each trait that it inherits. One of the genes is contributed by the sire and the other by the dam. Let's take an example, when, let's say, a black Cocker Spaniel is bred to a buff one. All of the first generation offspring will be black. Each parent contributed one gene for color to each hybrid offspring. One parent, obviously one that produces black color, contributed a "factor" for black color while the other parent passed along a "factor" for buff.

Obviously, the ability in this breed for black to overshadow buff is dominant over the tendency to produce buff color, which we can call recessive. The recessive characteristic was the hidden or masked one that did not appear in the offspring.

A dog, again using as an illustration the buff color in Cocker Spaniels, can show a recessive trait only when both factors (genes) are present in the same individual. The dominant trait will appear when one or both dominant genes are present.

To clarify matters a bit, let's see what happens when one of the black first generation hybrid specimens is crossed with another just like it. In such a mating, the hybrids can pass on to each of their offspring either the black or buff characteristics. Therefore, the transmission of one or the other factor has a fifty-fifty chance. Remember, these are hybrid specimens which have a black (dominant) gene and a buff (recessive) gene. Let's symbolize them as B-dominant, b-recessive. Since the combination is random, the ways in which these can be combined in a

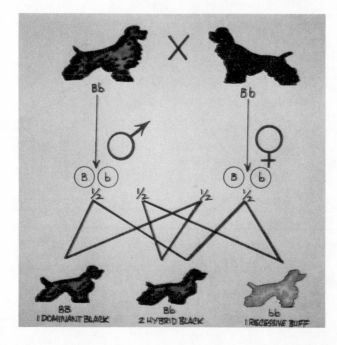

42

hybrid/hybrid cross are illustrated. As shown, it is possible to predict not only the possible combinations of factors, but also the probability for each of the combinations.

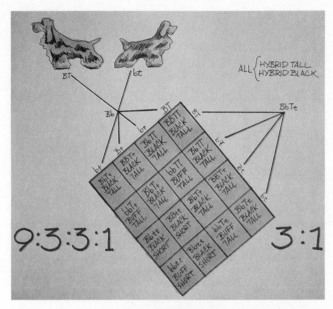

Chance plays a part in both the biological and physical worlds. By chance, we mean events that happen at random. Mendel was aware of this and knew something of the laws of probability. He used these in explaining his results, saying we should be wary of interpreting the occurrence of a single random event. However, he went on to point out that if large numbers of occurrences of the same event take place at random, there is a kind of order in the result in spite of the uncertainty of the occurrence of a single event. Wow! That's quite a mouthful.

Now let's move from the inheritance of a single trait to the inheritance of two traits simultaneously.

Having bred a (pure) black that is tall (also pure) to a short buff specimen that is also pure for its traits, we will get tall black offspring, since those traits are dominant. The offspring will be like the black parent.

Now, when you take these hybrid offspring, which are hybrid tall/hybrid black, and mate them with similar specimens, the resultant types are quite interesting. There will be four different types produced. As you see, there is a small black type and tall buff type. These types were new combinations of the two traits.

Continuing in this vein, and for all other traits as well, the distribution ratio turns out to be 9:3:3:1. This means that for every nine tall black dogs in a hybrid/hybrid mating there will be three tall dogs with buff coats, three small dogs with black coats, and one short buff specimen.

A quick glance will show twelve tall dogs to four short ones and twelve black dogs to four buff ones. Both

demonstrate the 3:1 ratio already established for the inheritance of a single trait in which segregation occurs.

In breeding for color in a dog, we find that the majority of factors which determine coat color appear to be "single factors," inherited according to Mendel's Laws. However, many of these color factors are influenced by other genes which have the ability to modify the expression of the "key" gene in numerous ways and thus account for

considerable variation in the finished product. As an example, while a dog may possess "key" genes which have the ability to create the Black and Tan pattern and may, therefore, be a Black and Tan insofar as its genetic makeup is concerned, independent modifying genes may alter its appearance by restricting or by allowing full expression of the tan pigment in its coat, so that it looks like a black dog or a tan dog.

Though the color of a dog's coat may be determined by a single gene or by a pair of genes, the skeletal structure of a dog is determined by the interaction of a large number of genes. It should not be difficult to understand why something as highly complex as the structure of a dog's head or body is not controlled by the action of a single hereditary factor or pair of factors.

Take movement, for example. Needless to say, there is no one gene labeled "gait" which has the ability to determine whether an individual puppy will move properly or improperly. Rather, there are countless genes, working in harmony or against each other, which determine these facts.

When we seek to determine the manner in which any part of an animal's skeletal structure is inherited, we are not dealing with single-factor inheritance, but with multiple-factor inheritance.

Any attempt to explain multiple-factor inheritance fully at this point would be utterly confusing to most people. However, the following facts may serve to give you a better understanding of this complex subject:

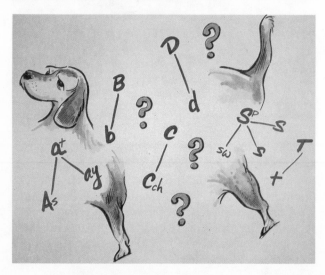

1. What we see and describe as a single character (a leg, foot, tail, etc.) is often affected and influenced in its development by a large number of different and unrelated genes which are capable of independent assortment.

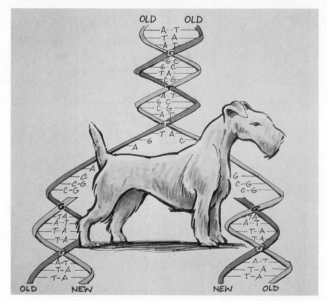

2. It is extremely difficult to sort out the various genes which influence a particular character, and to determine the specific effect each gene has on that character. In other words, just how important is the part which each gene plays in the development of that particular character?

3. Some genes have a direct, complete influence on the development of a character. They are called dominant genes. Some have only a partial effect, being neutralized to some extent by the action of the opposite members of the pair. They are called incompletely dominant genes. Some genes are completely masked and have no effect unless such genes comprise both members of a given pair. They are called recessive genes. In the study of any given character, only careful records obtained on a large scale will throw light on the difference between these types of hereditary action and influence.

4. The combination of multiple gene effects joined with environmental influences is the rule rather than the exception in such characteristics as body length, height, weight, and head and muzzle development. As an example, it has been found that body size depends upon some genes that affect all the tissues and upon others that influence only certain regions, such as the legs, neck, or tail. Then, in addition, diet, exercise, and other environmental influences determine to some extent the degree to which genes are able to stimulate and produce growth of the different tissues, organs, and body parts.

Of the one hundred and twenty-eight breeds eligible for registration by The American Kennel Club, none is purebred in the true sense of the word; that is, all of them are subject to variations of form and type which may

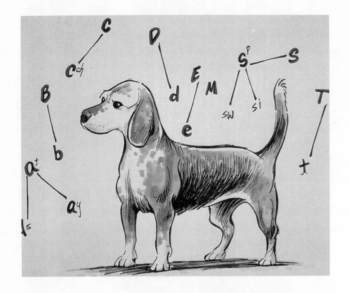

account for considerable differences in appearance between specimens of the same breed. Unlike certain strains of laboratory mice, which have been standardized by inbreeding and selection, and which are like peas in a pod, no breed of dog exists which reproduces its own kind without variations or differences, which may be either slight or considerable in degree.

It is probable that the major differences which exist between breeds are due to independent genes which may be found in one breed and not in another. Therefore, the manner in which the multiple hereditary factors responsible for the construction of an Afghan's body are inherited, may differ from the manner in which the countless genes which build a Boxer's body are inherited. If breeders really want to know more about the manner in which such complex parts as the body, legs, head, and other structural parts are inherited, the following will be necessary:

1. Observations of a large number of animals, resulting in careful and accurate records of the differences in structure which exist within the breed.

2. Accurately recorded breeding tests between animals of contrasting structural types, and recorded observations of their resulting offspring. This may well require the crossing of breeds at one or more genetic research laboratories. In this way, extreme types can be compared and the inheritance of marked differences in structure can be studied.

3. The making available of these records to scientists who are qualified to analyze them. Obviously, the task of breeding and raising enough animals representing different breeds, and recording their structural types and the types of their offspring, is beyond the finances and ability of any one person or any one institution. However, such data could be collected by breeders at no additional expense and with only a small amount of additional work. Each breeder's records could be sent to a central location at a scientific laboratory for tabulation and analysis and any resulting conclusions could, in turn, be made available to breeders.

Many breeders we talked with have practiced line breeding, but only skirted around the edges of inbreeding, having shied away from carrying it to its full fruition. From our reading we found out that as a means of finding which animals have the best genes, inbreeding seems to deserve more use than it has yet received. Not only does it uncover recessives more surely than any other method, but also it increases the relationship between the inbred animal and its parents and other relatives, so that the animal's pedigree and the merits of the family to which it belongs become more dependable as indicators of its own genes than can be the case with animals which are not inbred.

Considerable inbreeding is necessary if family selection is to be very effective. As we have learned, the gene is the unit of inheritance, but the animal is the smallest unit which can be chosen or rejected for breeding purposes. To breed exclusively from one or two of the best specimens available would tend to fix their qualities, both good and bad. In fact, that is the essence of what happens in extreme inbreeding. Moreover, the breeder will make at least a few mistakes in estimating which animals have the very best inheritance. Hence, in a practical program, the breeder will hesitate to use even a very good stud too extensively.

The breeder also is far from having final authority to decide how many offspring each of his bitches will produce. Some of his basic stock may die or prove to be sterile, or will be prevented by a wide variety of factors from having as many get as the breeder wants. Bitches from which he wants a top stud dog may persist in producing only females for several litters. Consequently, some specimens from which he really did not want so many offspring leave more to make up for the offspring he does not get from the dog he prefers.

The ideal plan for the most rapid improvement of the

breed may differ from the plan of the individual breeder, chiefly in that he dare not risk quite so much deterioration as may result from inbreeding. If the object were to improve the breed with little regard for immediate show prospects, then it would be a different story. Let's go into this in greater detail.

As we know, inbreeding refers to the mating of two closely related individuals. Most breeders practice inbreeding to a limited extent, even though they may term it close line breeding—for example, the breeding of half brother to half sister, father to daughter, and son to mother, is really inbreeding. Most breeders probably consider these three categories as representative of true inbreeding.

As neophyte breeders, we were in no position to advocate or condemn the practice of inbreeding, but, rather, to ascertain what it can and cannot accomplish. We will attempt to present what we learned and dispel some common fallacies.

It certainly would be interesting to know exactly what percentage of inbreeding does take place in various breeds and what results are obtained. Speaking in generalities, it would probably be safe to say that only a very small percentage of all champions were the products of inbreeding (brother/sister, father/daughter, son/mother), and perhaps that is being generous. On this basis, one would reasonably conclude that the practice of inbreeding on these terms is relatively rare.

In the breeding of domestic animals, such as cattle, chickens, etc., as well as in plant breeding, inbreeding is regarded as a most valuable tool to fix a desired type and purify a strain. Scientific experiments have proven this to be a fact. This raises the question of why inbreeding has not gained more widespread acceptance among dog breeders. By combining inbreeding with the selection of those individuals most nearly ideal in appearance and temperament, the desired stability of the stock is quickly obtained.

The mating of brothers and sisters probably is most likely to produce inbreeding degeneration. This is because a brother/sister mating is the most intense form of inbreeding. Studies show that those breeders who have attempted to cross full brothers and sisters, for the purpose of fixing good characteristics in their stock, give very contradictory reports of their results. One will often find that the mating of brother and sister results in somewhat decreased vitality and robustness in the offspring.

It may happen that abnormal or stillborn individuals are segregated out of the litter if special weakening genes are carried in the stock. On the other hand, it is just as certain that one can be fortunate enough to avoid inbreeding degeneration. Everything depends upon the hereditary nature of the animals concerned. Inbreeding degeneration is of such a peculiar nature that it may be totally abolished by a single crossing with unrelated or distantly related animals. However, if inbreeding degeneration had made its appearance, the breeder should know it was present in the hereditary make-up of his stock.

The theoretical rate at which continued brother/sister matings increase genetic alikeness has been calculated by a number of investigators. (The most reliable calculations at hand indicate the reduction in the proportion of unlike gene pairs closely approximates 19.1 percent per generation after the first generation, in which the reduction is 25 percent.) This rate is so rapid that after ten generations of brother/sister matings, starting with specimens that are 50 percent alike, about 94 percent of all gene pairs are alike. Therefore, such inbreeding produces its greatest effect during the *earlier* generations and has relatively little effect if continued beyond ten to twelve generations.

What does all this mean for us in relation to breeding good dogs? From the foregoing data, several conclusions are obvious. These traits may be good or they may be undesirable, depending entirely upon the individual's hereditary nature. Inbreeding creates *nothing new*—it merely *intensifies* what is already present. If the hereditary nature of an individual contains undesirable traits, these will naturally be manifested when the recessive genes become regrouped and fixed. This applies to the desirable traits as well.

Let's see if we can clarify a concept. The term *genotype* refers to the invisible genetic make-up of an individual, in contrast to the apparent, or visible, type of the individual, which is called *phenotype*. In selecting puppies to retain for breeding stock, breeders must rely on phenotype because they have no way of knowing an unproven individual's genotype. Inbreeding can reduce genotype and phenotype to one common denominator.

Suppose that an outstanding specimen appears which is the product of inbreeding. What would this mean in terms of breeding? It would mean that this specimen has a greater chance of passing on his visible traits rather than possible hidden traits. Prepotent dogs and bitches are usually those that are pure for many of their outstanding characteristics. Since only a limited amount of inbreeding has been carried on in most breeds, prepotent specimens have become pure for certain traits more or less *by chance*, for they have appeared in all breeds as products of outcrossing, as well as by line breeding.

Since line breeding, and especially close line breeding, is a limited form of inbreeding, the same good and bad points apply to line breeding, but in much more modified degree. The practice of inbreeding appears to be extremely limited in dogs, so one must assume that breeders are willing to trade slower progress for a lower element of risk.

To clarify what we have learned so far, let's take some practical examples and see what we can learn from them. It has been determined that any given bitch is to be either line bred or outcrossed and the proper stud dog which complements her has been selected. The breeding has been made, the puppies arrive, are tenderly watched over, and begin to grow up. Hopefully, it is indeed a good breeding, and the results yield several good prospects, all carrying the dam's good traits and showing great improvement in the areas where she needed help. But, what if it doesn't turn out that way? What if the breeding results in general disappointment with none of the puppies showing much improvement? The breeder might ask how this can possibly happen when all the proper aspects were taken into consideration in planning this breeding.

Remember the concept of "dominance"? Test breeding is the only true way of determining whether a dog or bitch is especially dominant. Here again, line breeding comes into play, for the closely line-bred dog or bitch has a much better chance of being dominant by virtue of a concentrated bloodline than the dog or bitch that is not line bred. When selecting a stud to complement a bitch, it is important to take into serious consideration the qualities of his parents as well. For example, suppose a stud is sought to improve the bitch's head quality. Obviously, a dog with a beautiful head is chosen, but it is also important that his parents have beautiful heads as well. Then, the stud can be considered to be "homozygous" for this trait. If the dog selected does not have parents with beautiful heads, or only one parent has a beautiful head, he is said to be "hererozygous" for this characteristic, and his chance of reproducing it are diminished. Dominant dogs and bitches are homozygous for more of their traits, while less dominant dogs and bitches are primarily heterozygous.

The great majority of dogs and bitches are probably dominant for some of their traits and not especially dominant for others. It is up to the breeder to attempt to match up the proper combination of dominant traits, which is why the dog and bitch should complement each other—that being the best practical way of attempting to come up with the right combinations. There are some dogs and bitches that are completely non-dominant in their genetic make-up, so when bred to a dominant partner, good things result provided that partner is of top quality.

It is obvious, then, that a number of dogs and bitches in a breed have become producers, when, in reality, *they did everything but really produce.* But when a non-dominant bitch is bred to a non-dominant stud, the litter is bound to be a disappointment. As we mentioned earlier, when a dominant bitch is bred to a dominant stud, it is also possible that the resulting litter will be a failure. This explains why some "dream breedings" result in puppies which do not compare in quality with either parent.

There are some dominant sires which, in turn, pass on the ability to their sons which also, in turn, pass on their producing ability to their sons, etc. Likewise, there are dominant bitches which pass on their producing ability to their daughters, granddaughters, great granddaughters, etc. Thus, some lines are noted for their outstanding producing sires and/or bitches. Such lines are true "producing bloodlines." To be more specific, a producing bitch (usually with a heritage of producing bitches behind her) bred to a proven stud dog will usually come through with those sought-after champion offspring. Now that's what *we* want.

Much discussion between breeders has centered on the subject of which parent contributes the most, the sire or the dam. As we have read, each contributes fifty percent of their genetic heritage; but by so doing, their respective factors of dominance and recessiveness are brought into play. Thus, in reality, there is not an equal contribution, for if there were, there would be *no outstanding producers.*

Armed with this knowledge, we spoke to a number of sincere old-timers in the breed to make sure we could combine practical knowledge with theory, and when we felt we were ready, we purchased those two good bitches.

The first one we purchased was from one of those old-time breeders. She was three years old and as the dam of two litters, was a proven producer. There was a champion in the first litter, and while none in her second litter were world beaters, they were all of good quality and were uniform in type. Breeding her to Rudolph would complement her general appearance but would not be close line breeding.

We purchased the second bitch, a year-old maiden, from Mrs. Moneypenny, Rudolph's breeder. This second bitch was good enough to show, and was a half-sister to Rudolph from the same dam.

Well, there you are—we were ready to set the world afire, and to think, not long before we had been carefree dogless wretches.

Puppies, Puppies—
Here They Come, Ready or Not

You guessed it. We bought a set of kennel plans, and after checking our local zoning laws, built an extension onto the rear of our garage. Then we moved Bitty and Greta into their runs and we were in the "business."

Bitty, the older bitch, came into season first and was bred to Rudolph on her thirteenth and fifteenth days (two services). She seemed willing on each occasion, and so was Rudolph.

While waiting for the bitches to come in season we spent a great deal of time reading articles on whelping and caring for puppies. We also visited with a nearby Doberman breeder, Burt, whom we had met at the shows. He had ten years of practical experience and we listened attentively to what he had to say.

Burt pointed out that in the beginning the objective should be to have the bitch in the very best possible physical condition before she is bred in order to maintain her health during the gestation period, so that her offspring will greet the world in the pink of condition. Four to six weeks in advance is not too soon. Have her checked thoroughly by a competent veterinarian for general condition: coat, development, the presence of internal parasites, possible anemia, etc. Then, if it is found that she is anemic, for example, measures should be taken right away to build her up so that she will be in prime condition. Internal parasites should be evacuated to the best of your ability. In other words, everything within your power should be done to get the bitch in A-one condition for her new responsibilities.

It is best to check for internal parasites again just prior to breeding the bitch. But if you belong to the "never do today what you can put off until she is in whelp" school, remember that the deadline for worming is within the first three weeks after the bitch is bred. If you forgot it, then omit worming and gather gray hairs worrying over those wormy puppies.

In the early stages of pregnancy—that is, the first three weeks—a bitch requires very little extra care. Her diet must be a well-balanced one containing adequate quantities of protein, carbohydrates, fat, minerals, and vitamins. Meat, eggs, and milk contain the essential amino acids not necessarily found in prepared foods and vegetables, and should be the principal constituents of her diet. Cooked meat is preferable to raw, and vegetables should be fed either raw or slightly cooked in order to preserve valuable vitamins. Beef, liver, horsemeat, eggs, milk, and vegetables provide the necessary food substances and may be combined with various prepared cereals to round out a well-balanced diet for your bitch. As soon as Bitty was bred, we started her on a calcium preparation and vitamin D. Burt preferred a capsule, dicalcium phosphate with iron and vitamin D, one per day for the first four weeks, then two per day for the remainder of the period.

During the first to the third week, we fed Bitty twice daily, using her usual quantity of food but in divided feedings. After the third week we gradually doubled the quantity. After the seventh week, we fed her three times daily without increasing the quantity, so as not to over-distend her stomach at any one feeding. In the last twenty days, we stopped giving her hard-to-digest foods. In the last five days we made her diet slightly laxative in an attempt to help her eliminate extra waste products from her system. We added a pinch of sodium bicarbonate to the drinking water throughout the entire period but knew this was most essential during the last week. This has a tendency to reduce the danger of acid milk, which causes the death of not a few puppies. Starting three days before she was due to whelp, we gave her a teaspoonful of milk of magnesia each day to aid in the evacuation of waste from the intestinal tract.

During the first weeks we exercised her as usual. After the fifth week, we restricted any violent exercise such as fast and continuous running. Grace walked Bitty briskly twice daily on a lead.

Was she in whelp or not? We learned there is no sure early sign to ascertain whether or not a bitch is in whelp. Our vet told us the presence of puppies cannot be determined before four weeks, at which time they may be the size of hickory nuts. He said that by laying the bitch on her side facing us, placing one hand underneath with the other on top of the abdomen, and then moving the fingers gently along the abdomen, we might be able to feel the swollen tubes on each side. He said that the breasts begin to enlarge with milk content toward the end of the sixth week.

We were told that beginning about one week before the bitch is due to whelp, we should clean her teeth daily, using a mixture of table salt and sodium bicarbonate. This tends to lessen the possibility of navel and other infections in the newborn puppies. We were told to keep the bitch's skin as free as possible from eczema, lice, fleas, and ticks, but to not use insecticides late in the pregnancy.

About the fifty-seventh day from the first breeding, old Mother Nature gave us a few hints. Bitty's shape began to change. Instead of resembling a sausage, her weight shifted lower down in the body and her hip bones became quite prominent. Her nipples began to swell and we were able to express milk from them.

About one week before Bitty was due, we bathed her thoroughly, giving special attention to cleaning her breasts. We picked out a place for whelping which was quiet and out of the way, in our utility room. With my "great" carpenter's talent, I built a whelping box, and for a week before the puppies were due, I encouraged Bitty to

sleep in it so that she would become accustomed to it. Not Bitty—she wouldn't go near it. I made it of sufficient size to house Bitty and her puppies, and raised it slightly off the floor to avoid drafts and to facilitate cleaning the box. We gathered the other supplies which would be needed: a good-sized stack of clean newspapers, clean but expendable towels, sterile scissors, cotton, tincture of merthiolate, baby oil, sterile thread, pencil, writing paper, scale, alcohol (for sterilizing and cleaning scissors), a fairly

small cardboard box (obtained at the supermarket but we made sure it hadn't contained insecticides), hot water bottle or heating pad, and brandy and an eyedropper for stimulating the sluggish puppy. We gathered these supplies and set them out beforehand so that they would be available immediately when needed. We lined the whelping box with many thicknesses of newspaper so that Bitty could utilize her instinct to make a nest if she was so inclined. We also had a container for the disposal of waste.

At last the time seemed right. Bitty's temperature dropped to 97.5 at ten a.m. and from what we had learned from experienced breeders, the puppies would come at any time in the next twelve hours. Grace phoned me frantically at the office and said I had to get home at once. Ha! Easier said than done. It would have to happen on a day when I had a corporate buyer in and an important meeting with the vice-president for finance. Besides, it was only the sixty-first day. How could she do this to me?

I thought as fast as my numbed brain would allow and came up with the lame excuse that I had a very upset stomach and needed to get home at once. Leaving this lame excuse for my secretary to communicate to the higher-ups, I took my cowardly leave of absence. Anyone seeing me sprint for my car surely would have believed my excuse.

After a harrowing forty-five minute trip home, during which I ran two red lights and drove like a man on his way to an accident, I arrived home expecting to see a whole litter of puppies. Instead, there was Bitty sleeping at Grace's feet and giving no indication of any action. I didn't know whether to gnash my teeth or be thankful all was well. As long as there wasn't any action, we started to make plans for a leisurely lunch. Just then Bitty gave a loud yelp, jumped two feet into the air, and came down with a puzzled look on her face. She kept peering behind her and then up at us, as if to ask, "What's going on here?" Bitty then began to pace around the room and to pant heavily. From our readings, and from the water spreading around her, we knew enough to realize that serious action might be coming now.

We double-checked our whelping equipment and put another layer of paper in the whelping box. As we ran hither and yon, Bitty looked at us as if she doubted our sanity. Her look seemed to say, "What can you expect from these novices? They are totally disorganized." I glared right back at her—after all, she hadn't yet gone near the whelping box. She would walk up to it, sniff around, flounce her tail, and walk away disdainfully. Who did she think she was, the Queen of Sheba? I had spent days working from a set of plans putting that thing together. Now what did I have to show for it? A haughty bitch and two bashed fingernails. Nuts to her!

After lunch, after dinner, after a midnight snack—still no puppies. Her temperature was still about 97.5. At times she actually hopped into the whelping box and dug up the papers and hopped out again. Most of the time she seemed content to lie at Grace's feet. Grace did remind me that so far this behavior was okay, and she had called the vet right after she had called me, asking him to stand by. That was consoling.

At 3:30 a.m., as the last rerun of "Father Knows Best" was concluding and Robert Young was solving another major family crisis, Bitty decided it was time to get down to business.

She sauntered into the whelping box and began to tear up paper better than the shredder I had at the office. She snorted like a little pig seeking acorns and twirled around and around. It was quite a performance. She sure had me convinced she meant business.

About twenty minutes later something began to come out of the vagina. It looked gray, black, and slimy. Just as we positioned ourselves to help, it disappeared. Hey, what was going on? Bitty just sat there and looked up at us. For the next half hour she just sat there with a glazed look in her eyes. Then she started bearing down again and having major contractions. Out came this thing again. Just as fast, it retreated again. Don't get me wrong, we knew a little bit about whelping from our "get smart" period of visiting with other breeders and reading, but no one had told us about this hide-and-go-seek business. While Bitty did her glazed-look bit again, we took time out for a conference.

"Look," said Grace, "obviously she is having trouble getting this puppy out. We need to help her."

"Ugh," I groaned, "can't we just watch and count on Mother Nature to help?"

"No," said the wife, her eyes snapping, "we've got to help."

So, as Bitty began her next series of contractions, Grace leaned over the box and gently lifted Bitty's front legs up in the air over her knees and I grabbed this "thing," using a rough towel.

It was quickly evident that my first experience in whelping a litter was going to be a dilly, for I clearly had hold of a puppy's tail and back legs, a breach delivery (most puppies come head first). Oh boy! I gradually was able to work my fingers around the puppy and partially up inside the vagina and began a slow, easy, turning motion to ease it out. Bitty looked at me with a look which seemed to confirm her earlier opinion. I was in no mood to be talked down to, so I told her to keep her opinions to herself and to help by pushing down hard. You know, she was brighter than I thought because she did just that. The only problem was, I wasn't ready for it. As I tugged, the puppy came barreling out and I plopped back on my keister with a thud. Fortunately I hung onto the puppy. Eureka! We were breeders.

I put the puppy down and Bitty immediately broke the sac it was encased in and neatly nipped the umbilical cord. While she was doing this, a blue-green blob eased out of her vagina. This, we knew, was the afterbirth, and she quickly ate that. We watched as Bitty licked the puppy all over and tumbled it around the box. The puppy was making "fussing" noises and Bitty was the doting mother. After a few minutes she began to have additional contractions. We took the puppy and weighed it, made sure it had no water in its lungs, checked the sex (male) and put it in a little box that had the hot water bottle at the bottom and which was covered by a towel. We recorded the weight, the sex, and the time of birth on a three-by-five card we had prepared in advance.

It was now 4:30 a.m. Surprisingly, we weren't tired at all. I guess the old adrenaline was really flowing.

In my naivete and optimism I fully expected that now that she was started, the whole litter would be whelped by breakfast time and I could shower, shave, and get to my nine o'clock meeting. Think again! Bitty apparently thought her work was done. She popped out of the box, made a mess on the floor, and then went back to her favorite position at Grace's feet. She stretched, belched, and settled down for a snooze. I couldn't believe my eyes! Nowhere in the literature did it mention this kind of time out. Was there only one puppy? Was her uterus "pooped out"? Or was she just being a contrary female?

We decided not to panic since she did not seem uncomfortable, but to call the vet about breakfast time. Bitty slept on. We could see tremors shake her body but apparently not hard enough to cause her concern.

At 7:30 Grace called the vet, and being an understanding man, he didn't seem at all upset. He suggested that we set the one puppy to nursing, and that if there was no further action by 9:00 a.m., we bring Bitty to the clinic. The telephoning got Bitty's attention, for she got up, stretched, and strolled over to the whelping box, got inside, squatted, gave one big grunt, and out came another puppy. Then, in quick order, all within an hour, she had six more puppies. You figure it out!

We recorded all the pertinent information, made sure all the puppies were nice and dry and hooked on to a faucet, and then collapsed on the couch. We were truly tired now. Bitty looked up at us as if to say "Piece of cake." Ha! That was all right for her to say.

The puppies all seemed content to nurse and they looked uniform in size. After all the noses and other equipment were counted, we found we had six males and two bitches.

After assuring ourselves that all the puppies had been whelped, we forced Bitty to go outside to relieve herself, and Grace stayed with her in case another puppy should be whelped unexpectedly. We were prepared for the clear, red discharge which we were told would last about two weeks or so, diminishing gradually.

We then sponged off her underside and cleaned her up. I cleared away all the messy papers and put fresh, clean bedding in her box. We used toweling which provided a rough enough surface to give the puppies the needed traction to nurse. I knew enough to keep the bedding clean at all times.

After all the housekeeping chores were done we offered Bitty a light meal, and then allowed her to settle down so the puppies could nurse. She was keeping them clean, and their bodily processes functioning properly, by licking them.

We placed each puppy on a breast again and made sure all the puppies knew how to eat. This came naturally when they were headed in the right direction, toward the food supply. Two of them had to be shown how by actually placing the nipple in their mouths. (We made sure the tongue was under the nipple.)

You know, I fell asleep on the sofa right after that, and never did call the office to tell them I wouldn't be in. I hoped I had a job the next day. Oh well, who cared? I was truly in the dog game now.

Raising the Litter
or
They're Cute and Cuddly,
But What a Mess They Make

Guess what? The boss forgave me for not showing up at the office the day Bitty whelped. A very tolerant man, old B. J. Of course he implied I was going soft in the head to get tangled up with the dog breeding stuff, but he *was* forgiving.

Meanwhile, back at the O.K. Whelping Corral, Grace reported that all was well. Bitty was snuggled in comfortably and all the puppies were piled one on top of the other, sleeping peacefully. Their bellies appeared full, and none of them was crying or felt cold. So far, so good. One of the major things we had learned was to watch for any puppy that would wander away and get chilled. This could be dangerous. However, this gang seemed to believe in togetherness.

That evening, after I got home, we reviewed what we had been through, how we could do better next time, and what we had to look forward to with this litter.

First, we wanted to make sure that Bitty was okay, and we scheduled a trip to the vet the next day to have him check her out. Next, we wanted to set up a plan for weighing and measuring the puppies at specific intervals until they were eight weeks of age. Any that we kept would continue to be measured at three months, four months, six months, ten months, and one year. That way we could begin to have organized records that could help us in subsequent litters. With this system we hoped to be able to predict how certain puppies would develop, based upon solid statistics.

For the next few weeks all went well. Bitty kept the puppies well fed and clean and they were as quiet as church mice. About the tenth day some of them began to open their eyes and see the big world around them. By the fourteenth day all of them had their eyes open. There went the peace and quiet!

Now that they could see one another, they considered it a personal challenge if one puppy was struggling along up on its legs while the others were down. They would attack this upstart until it too came tumbling down. It then was a race to see which one could clamber to its feet first and start all over again. What snarls!

By the end of the fourth week Bitty was getting a bit tired of this full-time motherhood and was spending a great deal more time out of the box. Her usual response to the puppies' plaintive cries for food was to cock open one eye and then close it again. It was time to start weaning the puppies.

We figured Bitty had a good supply of milk and could provide all or most of the puppies' food for about five weeks. However, at this age, or even earlier, many breeders start weaning on finely crumbled, soft, moist dog meal, mixed with warm milk or water. We introduced this semi-solid food by putting it in a shallow pan for Bitty. Curiosity led the pups to investigate, usually feet first. They then proceeded to teach themselves to lap. Before feeding the puppies, we kept the bitch away from them for about an hour. They showed a greater interest when they were a little hungry. We gradually decreased the amount of liquid in the mixture as the pups got older, and of course increased the amount of food.

By eight weeks of age, they were accustomed to eating what should be their normal diet for the rest of their lives. With the puppies getting considerable nourishment from the semi-solid food, while still nursing, the drain on Bitty was considerably reduced. This enabled her to make a faster comeback after the puppies were weaned.

It was surprising how quickly the puppies learned to be clean. As soon as they could waddle, they went away from their sleeping place to relieve themselves. The pen was large enough, so we put a partition, two-inches high, in the middle, to make them use one part for sleeping and the other part as their exercise pen. This was a start toward paper-training and housebreaking.

We were now ready for some serious appraisals of the litter. In our sessions with some more experienced breeders, we learned that in comparing individual specimens, rather than groups, the greatest differences in body size and formation may arise through "internal environment"—chiefly glandular—which may be, in part, hereditary. The most striking examples, of course, are provided by the comparisons between dogs and bitches. Here, two physically distinct groups of dogs are produced through overall developmental differences set in motion by the sex chromosome balances, which cause the same inheritance to work in radically different ways.

Importantly, we learned that differences, which may be in part genetic, have been found in the rate of growth and development in different animals. Thus, some dogs that grow faster in one period may grow less than average during another period. Also important is the fact that heights in different dogs are achieved in different ways. In our study of heredity we found that some genes affect body development uniformly, whereas others specialize with respect to certain segments such as length of legs, shoulder placement (which has an outward effect on the appearance of height), etc. A good example is the comparison of two dogs measuring the same height. One may look tall, even bordering on "oversize," whereas the other may actually look low, with no appearance of "oversize."

We thought it would be desirable to be able to predict ultimate growth with some reliability. In addition, it would be just as desirable to have a scale by which development could be charted along with growth. In other words, approximately how large or how small should any puppy be at any given age, and what would be a desirable weight to go with its size? This is necessarily complex because of the many factors involved. When it comes to weight, heaviness of bone must be taken into consideration. Also, there must be some consideration of type.

We hoped that by recording accurately the weights and measurements of each puppy in every litter, a picture would begin to emerge. Of course, the fewer the bloodlines involved, the easier the task. The more data collected, the greater the basis for comparison. We knew the system of recording must be individual and consistent. In other words, measurements, for example, need not be official measurements so long as they are gathered and recorded in the same way each time. By way of illustration,

data to be recorded could include records of puppy weights and measurements at various ages. Measurements could be divided into different categories, such as measurement of height (floor to withers, floor to elbow, elbow to withers), and measurement of length (withers to tailset).

We figured that when that important puppy came along, we could refer back to our records gathered on previous puppies from that bloodline and utilize what the data told about the puppy. It would give us a reasonably good idea as to whether a current young hopeful was growing and developing as he should, compared to previous puppies, in order to bring out his ultimate potential.

Using this approach, we figured we should be able to come up with the answers to the following questions as they pertain to our own breeding stock:

1. Does size and weight of puppies at birth indicate size and weight at maturity?

2. What is the earliest possible age at which ultimate growth and/or development is predictable?

3. At what age is ultimate growth and/or development reached?

4. During what age period does the greatest rate of growth take place?

5. Is ultimate development correlated with ultimate growth, or is one attained before the other?

6. If diverse bloodlines are bred within the same kennel, what are the differences between them with respect to growth and development?

7. Is growth and/or development attained uniformly, or rather through sporadic leaps coupled with periods of quiescence?

8. Is growth and/or development attained at the same rate, or does one part grow and/or develop before another part?

Being a statistics nut, I thought it was quite possible that other interesting facts and ideas could become evident to me. We knew that by recording all of this data, we would become aware of what we were breeding. We thought it would be to our advantage to know and to understand all the various phases of growth and development in our bloodlines rather than place that promising puppy in the kennel without a second look until it grew up.

Well, believe it or not, Bitty raised her litter successfully. We kept one bitch, sold one dog at four months as a possible show specimen, and sold the others as nice quality pets.

Greta also was bred to Rudolph and whelped eight puppies. Fortunately, we were able to finish three champions out of these two breedings.

Greta and Bitty are old house matrons now, enjoying the good life. Bitty still questions many of my decisions but we have agreed to live and let live.

Since that time when our first litter was whelped, we have bred many others and have learned a good deal through practical experience. We would like to pass on to you much of what we have learned.

The development of any puppy is fascinating to observe. We found that no two develop in exactly the same way, yet there are definite similarities within the various bloodlines. This does not necessarily mean that all breeders engaged in breeding within a specific bloodline or combinations of that line will experience identical stages of development with respect to the growth of their puppies. It does mean, however, that certain similarities will exist, and the knowledge of these similarities will prove of great assistance to the individual breeder.

How any given puppy will look at maturity is predestined by its genetic heritage coupled with the environmental factors it experiences. Once the breeding has been made, the genetic heritage cannot be altered, although environmental factors can. However, the point of this discussion is how the puppy reaches maturity.

For example, it is well known that most puppies go through what is commonly termed the "awkward stage." The onset of this phase can be as early as eight weeks of age, and the phase can last until the puppy is eight months of age. We were told to pick the best ones when the puppies were eight weeks of age. This rule of thumb states that at this age puppies will show more indications of their adult potential than at any other age until they actually reach maturity.

This is well and good for puppies that actually follow the classic pattern mentioned above. However, not all puppies will fall into this category. There are many variations of the so-called awkward stage. The variations depend upon the different bloodlines involved and the individual differences within a bloodline which have been established through the process of individual selection. The latter will necessarily have a modifying effect on any specific bloodline, as will environmental influences, which will be dealt with later in this chapter.

Some puppies do not enter the awkward stage until they are three months old. Others don't enter it until four months. Some emerge by six months and others by seven or more months. There are some fortunate puppies that never go through the awkward stage at all. These fortunate puppies are often dubbed "flyers." They are outstanding at a very young age, and continue to be so classified on through maturity. Their less fortunate brothers and sisters may well emerge as equally outstanding in the final appraisal, even though they (and their breeders) had to endure the awkward stage. In light of all this, selection at eight weeks is not necessarily a rigid criterion you should use arbitrarily in making your selection. For the beginning breeder it may prove a useful rule, but as familiarity with development increases, it should be modified to meet the situation to which it is applicable.

Two primary conditions give rise to the awkward stage: one is the shedding of the baby teeth and the subsequent emergence of the adult teeth, and the other is a rapid rate of body growth. In some puppies the process of dentition creates a temporarily adverse effect upon head development. This is characterized by a cumulative "plaining out" period. Where the puppy once evidenced a deep stop, the foreface now appears to slide back into the skull like a ski slope. Most traces of chiseling disappear and the head becomes devoid of all embellishment. This is a trying period for any breeder, but one which must be endured. Just as the puppy's head began to fade gradually, so it usually begins to improve gradually as the puppy approaches maturity. Generally, the improvement becomes noticeable at about six months of age, and continues until the original head qualities have been restored.

In some cases, the original head qualities are never quite regained. A good indication that this might be the case is apparent during the plaining out period if the puppy loses its original squareness of muzzle or the skull appears to become broader than the muzzle. In other words, although the stop and chiseling all but disappear during the plaining out phase, the breeder can feel relatively assured that the head will revert to its original promise if it remains in balance during this period.

The plaining out phase can definitely be associated with characteristics of specific bloodlines within the breed. Some puppies never go through this phase. Their heads are good as tiny puppies and they continue to stay that way. This characteristic is also associated with specific bloodlines. In many instances breeders have been able to establish this trait in their stock through selective breeding.

Plainness of head and awkwardness of body do not necessarily go together, although they may. Ungainliness of body in the growing puppy can be likened to the stage experienced by the teenager when he is all arms and legs and lacking in fine coordination. Another adage commonly applied to this phase of development states that all puppies that will eventually evidence good size will go through this period, and, conversely, that those puppies that are destined eventually to be small adults will grow in proportion and not evidence the awkward body characteristics. There necessarily are exceptions to this rule.

Awkward body characteristics can take many different forms. Some puppies go up on leg at a very early age and look as if they are walking around on stilts until their bodies begin to develop depth and breadth. Others will develop first through the body and will appear low and dumpy until they begin to get their leg growth. Sometimes

different parts of the dog's body will grow at different rates, giving rise to the up-in-the-rear, down-at-the-shoulder, long-in-the-body looks that were not apparent at an earlier age and will not be apparent at maturity.

Some of these developmental changes may not disappear—that is, some dogs upon maturity will lack body development, others may be low on the legs, some will lack the correct top line, and others will be irrevocably long-backed. Of such things are faults made, of such things are disappointments born, and of such things do show prospects fade away. However, the appearance of these traits during one phase of body growth does not necessarily mean that they will be evident upon maturity. Almost all body characteristics are subject to change. Some puppies have been known to develop heavy shoulders during the awkward stage, and subsequently the shoulders have smoothed out. Steep shoulders have been known to lay back, etc. It is almost impossible to state with assurance that a specific trait is not subject to change, for there will always be some breeder who has experienced that change in his stock.

As beginning breeders with our first young hopefuls, we experienced many periods of dejection and frustration as the puppies grew and developed. By the time our second litter of hopefuls arrived, we were more assured in our minds as to their eventual conformation. And our assurance increased until we became fairly positive in our approach. Even experienced breeders are subjected to periods of dejection and frustration. It is often during these periods that wrong decisions are made, the wrong puppy is sold for a pet, or the wrong puppy is retained as a show and/or breeding prospect.

We found that even experienced breeders outcrossing into a new bloodline or obtaining new stock were subject to this disquieting situation. All they learned with regard to their own stock sometimes was subject to complete revision as they incorporated the new.

I guess it would be quite simple if it could be stated, for example, that all puppies from X bloodlines plain out in head at three months of age. Then breeders with puppies from X bloodlines would not become unduly dejected when their puppies entered this stage. This, of course, is not possible, for there are too many exceptions, individual differences, and environmental factors to be taken into account. It should be possible to say, however, that many puppies from X bloodlines do plain out in head about three months of age, and, therefore, should it happen, the breeder should not be unduly concerned, for the good characteristics will usually come back by, say, seven months of age. Armed thus, the breeder can bear this phase with patience and hope.

The same can apply to developmental stages of other body traits, and it therefore behooves breeders to take all of this into account. It is natural for a breeder to evaluate his own puppies in comparison with those of a fellow breeder, but in making such an evaluation a breeder is exposed to many pitfalls. One breeder may feel that, at any given age, his puppies are far superior to those of another breeder, a fact which may not hold true upon subsequent maturity of the puppies in question. It is unlikely that a breeder will be cognizant of the different developmental phases of another breeder's puppies, and therefore he may make his judgment on inapplicable criteria.

Most young show prospects do not live up to their original potential. The prospective buyer should realize or be made to realize that it is impossible for any breeder to predict ultimate development with absolute certainty. The majority of eight-week-old show prospects do not make the grade, and as each month passes, their ranks become thinner and thinner.

In an earlier chapter we reported on the size of the dog game. Therefore, it should come as no surprise to learn that every year hundreds of thousands of puppies are whelped in this country. Of these, thousands are tagged as possible show prospects by their breeders. Of these, only a small percentage ever are entered in shows, to say nothing of the few that actually finish their championships.

What has happened to cause the others to fall by the wayside? Some of the answers are obvious. For example, as they grow, many puppies develop undesirable traits which were not discernible at an earlier age but which were, nevertheless, predestined by their genetic heritage. What about the others, those which do not evidence obvious faults but which, upon maturity, seem to be lacking that certain something? Unfortunately, some of the qualities necessary for the prospective show winner are hard to describe, especially those qualities that have little or nothing to do with conformation. Among them are health, condition, personality, and disposition. These qualities must be developed to their ultimate potential in order to bring out the best in any puppy.

In order for any young show specimen to fulfill its early promise, its environment must provide it with all the necessary conditions to ensure its ultimate growth and development, both physical and mental. The person responsible for providing such an environment is, of course, the breeder or the owner. The owners of our first show prospect displayed all the mistakes new owners make, because they lacked know-how. Often it is through initial mistakes that the realization sets in that there is more to raising a good puppy than providing food and medical care. In addition, conditions may arise over which the breeder or owner has little control—illness, for example.

In the very beginning, a puppy's first contact with the world can have an important effect upon its later life. Beautiful though they may be, some bitches are poor mothers. They do little to get their puppies off to a good start. Other factors, as well, may be responsible for getting a puppy off to a poor start. However, puppies which do not get off to a good start, through no fault of their own, will usually catch up with those which are more fortunate, providing they are normal and healthy. They may not grow as quickly, and their growing period will usually be longer, but by the time they reach maturity, there should be little difference in actual size.

The same premise usually holds true for the older puppy which has received a setback due to illness. Its growth may be halted temporarily during an illness, but such puppies have been known to make up that period of growth at a later date. Many breeders are tempted to discard puppies such as these, and many do, only to find out later that they made a mistake.

The quantity and quality of food a puppy receives is very important. Poor nutrition can result in a puppy's failure to live up to its potential. The limits of a puppy's eventual size, bone, and development have been predestined by heredity. Even though these limits have been predetermined, they either can be developed to their maximum or never reached because of poor nutrition.

Eating is often a habit, and the so-called "good doers" are one step ahead in developing their potential. Through its own lack of effort the "poor doer" may be penalized regardless of nutritional opportunities provided. One of the most difficult tasks imaginable is to get the "poor doer" to develop properly. Any possible physical causes of lack of appetite, such as infected tonsils, worms, etc., should be investigated thoroughly. Unfortunately, there are some puppies that will never eat more than what is required for marginal sustenance.

The puppy that is a good eater will often be on the chubby, roly-poly side. Should it go through the awkward stage, its awkwardness will be more pronounced than that of its slimmer litter mates. The chubby puppy is the one which usually loads up in shoulder or which looks soft in back, sloppy, and cumbersome. The unknowing owner gives up on this specimen and discards it before a diet has had a chance to work wonders. Of course, you need to be aware that extreme obesity can cause permanent structural faults. At the other extreme, the too-thin puppy, while retaining a semblance of its original promise, often indicates that it will never "body out" enough to amount to anything. This puppy will often appear unthrifty, for the actual lack of nutrition can easily have an adverse effect on physical well being. This puppy, too, is often discarded without the owner attempting to ascertain the causes of its lack of appetite.

Another factor that should be mentioned in connection with nutrition is the ability of the puppy to utilize that with which it is provided. Some puppies are limited by physical abnormalities in the utilization of the nutriments provided, appetite notwithstanding.

Obviously, condition and tone will mark the healthy puppy which has the advantage of proper nutrition and which utilizes it to the fullest capacity. Barring undesirable hereditary factors, its coat will be shiny and will develop commensurately with age. Cleanliness and frequent grooming are also important. Dirty, matted puppies may grow coat but usually will not retain it.

In breeds where an outgoing personality and good disposition are highly desirable, the breeder must be conscious of his responsibility in helping such a personality to grow. It has often been said that a show specimen must have something more than mere physical beauty. Some have called this additional, rather obscure factor, "heart." Call it what one may, this extra "something" falls into the classification of personality and disposition.

Without some spark of personality, something which makes the dog an individual in its own right, the most perfect specimen is nothing but a shell. As for a bad disposition, nothing could be more of a detriment to a breed. Taking for granted that no inherited factors are involved, the responsibility for developing personality and disposition is just as important as providing food and medical care. The vast majority of shy, snapping, wetting puppies can usually trace their ills to environmental factors rather than to inherited ones.

Dogs which are to be shown must possess a certain sophistication not necessarily required by the more sheltered pet. New situations, strange people, and unusual noises must all be taken in stride and met with equanimity.

The puppy which is kept like the proverbial hothouse flower and which has never encountered different situations, can hardly be expected to react in an unruffled manner when suddenly confronted with a new and different type of challenge. Some might react with panic and others may meet the situation by withdrawing.

Personality development should start at a very early age—in fact, the earlier the better. Just as human babies thrive on tender loving care, so do puppies. As wee babies, they should be handled, petted, and loved. As they grow older, they will surely benefit from being played with, introduced to new situations, and offered the opportunity of human affection.

The manner in which a puppy is played with is very important. On the surface, the idea of playing with a puppy sounds like the simplest thing imaginable, but many breeders cringe inwardly while watching inexperienced people play with puppies. Some of the common pitfalls encountered are suddenly grabbing or lunging at a puppy, teasing, and even picking up the puppy in an improper way. The whole idea of playing with a puppy is to get across the idea to the puppy that it is doing something enjoyable and that this enjoyment is dependent upon the puppy's relationship with a human being, or with other puppies, as the case may be.

Last, but certainly not least, one must use common sense in raising puppies. Love them, play with them, but don't smother them. If you do you will have a spoiled brat on your hands. Besides, you don't want them to talk back to you as Bitty did, do you?

The Making and Training of a Judge

Twelve years have now gone by since we became players in the dog game. Rudolph is sitting at home, a fat and sassy thirteen-year-old with enough glory to last us a lifetime. He has sired nineteen champions, and others are being campaigned.

Grace and I, under our kennel prefix of Wunder Kind, have now bred eleven champions and have shown two of them ourselves. I have judged a number of sanctioned matches and sweepstakes and loved every minute of it. I guess I am a natural-born ham.

Members of our local club have been urging me to judge at licensed shows and I am wavering. I'm not quite sure I am fully ready to try my wings in a regular point show.

Grace knew of my reluctance and suggested that I talk to an all-rounder, a judge who can judge most of the breeds, so that I could get a more intimate picture of what a judge looks for, how he handles his ring, and any other insights that might be helpful in making my decision.

Since I really was serious, I thought very carefully about whom to ask for advice. I finally chose Izzy Schoenwulff, a noted old-timer whose judging I admired.

Once my decision was made, I barreled forward full speed. Izzy was most happy to talk with me, and arrangements were made to fly down to his place the following week.

He met me at the airport when I arrived and drove me out to his place for dinner. He is a remarkable man. He must be eighty if he is a day, and he gets around the ring like a man of forty-five. He also has a remarkable memory.

After dinner, he leaned back in his chair and delivered one of the best dissertations on judging I have ever heard. With his permission I tape recorded the session, and these are his comments, with only personal references left out.

"At the outset, let me clarify the role of a judge. A judge is primarily an educator to the exhibitor and spectator alike. Judges are also evaluators of the quality of the animals which are exhibited under them. As teachers, judges have to help the exhibitor learn that temperament, soundness, movement, and condition all play very important roles in the final placement.

"First and foremost, let me emphasize that it is especially important to judge the whole dog and not its individual parts. The total makeup of the dog, including breed type, gait, structure, and temperament should be before your eyes as you make decisions. *Do not,* I repeat, *do not,* judge by fault finding.

"Next, as the final arbiter in the ring, you should strive to place dogs that show balance—by that is meant dogs whose parts interrelate and interact. A beautiful, but huge, head is out of proportion on a small frame.

"A third cardinal point is moderation. Be cautious of dogs that emphasize extremes in any breed. Most Standards do not promote extremes.

"Yet another point is ring presence. You have been selected by AKC to officiate. Your control and command of the ring and your ability to make educated decisions in reasonable time is often the basis upon which the AKC representative and the gallery evaluate your performance.

"Another point is consistency. Breed types vary. With reasonable size entries, you should be able to select a breed type to your liking and stay with it. There are times when your winners will be 'different' because of the presence of an outstanding specimen of a different type. That's okay. Don't be rigid. Put up that outstanding specimen. However, as a general rule, stick to type.

"The dogs you select should be sound—meaning that they should be free of any disability. The term is usually applied to gait. A dog moving correctly, according to its breed Standard, is generally referred to as a sound dog.

"By all means, look for a dog in top condition which is neither too fat nor too lean. He should show good care, with a full coat having a natural luster.

"If you aspire to being a judge some day, take the time to read and study thoroughly the Standards of the breeds for which you wish to apply. Attend as many shows as possible. Watch the judges' actions as well as their placements. Watch their hands as they go over the dogs. See if their placements are consistent as to breed type. Compare your assessments against theirs. Watch all the dogs in a class, not just those you have singled out as best. Then think—while best for this class, is it the best dog for the breed?

"Steward at numerous shows and don't limit yourself to just your own breeds. It is amazing what you will learn from other breeds. Attend as many judging seminars as possible. They are great training opportunities.

"I am assuming that you have the proper knowledge of anatomy and gait, so we won't go into that.

"I want to concentrate on the 'how to's' of being a judge, and then I want to make you aware of how a judge can influence the direction a breed takes. Building on your knowledge of anatomy and motion, I will focus on breed type as the other end of the teeter-totter.

"Webster's defines type as 'qualities common to a number of individuals that serve to distinguish them as an identifiable class or kind'—qualities that are felt to indicate excellence in members of a group.

"Oftentimes we have heard certain dogs referred to as 'Eastern' in type, and others as 'Western' in type. A group of California dogs are automatically referred to as 'Western,' regardless of the bloodlines and/or appearance, and the same holds true of a group of New England dogs. Automatically they are called 'Eastern.'

"Let us assume there are in most breeds two or three distinct 'types' that are not restricted to any geographical area. Actually, it is rare to see the extremes of any one type, since within that type there are many variations and degrees. We are not talking about specific traits such as beautiful heads, long necks, extreme toplines, etc., but rather the general outline of the dog.

"Specific traits, however, do seem to go with certain types. For example, one of the truisms in American Cockers is that an extremely long neck and a short body just do not go together. Another is that an overdone head with lots of muzzle tends to produce throatiness.

"The two extreme types in Cockers are basically a streamlined dog and a blocky dog. The streamlined dog is often termed 'racy.' He is well up on leg with a long, well-arched neck, and usually exhibits some length of body—in proportion, however. Along with this, he is nicely boned but usually does not excel in bone and substance. The streamlined dog is slower to develop and is in his prime at three or four years of age. In addition, he tends to excel in topline and rear angulation. With this excellent topline can come a slightly Terrier-like front with poor forechest development.

"The blocky dog is just that in appearance. He is not overly large, as a rule, for he does not possess the height at the withers. His shoulders tend to lay back further. He is heavier-boned, with a good deal of rib spring and substance. His neck is shorter and thicker, but he is also shorter-backed. He gives the impression of being very sturdy.

"There appear to be specific characteristics that are both likely and unlikely to show up in certain types of dogs. These characteristics seem to be apparent regardless of the breed or bloodlines involved. In other words, it would almost seem that certain faults as well as certain desirable traits are linked closer to type, rather than being credited to specific bloodlines. It may well be that certain bloodlines produce a higher percentage of one type over another.

"The relationship between faults and/or desired traits with type could be due mainly to linkage. Linkage is a tendency of certain characteristics to appear together in heredity because the genes for these characteristics are located on the same chromosome. Sometimes two or more characteristics which are linked together are good, such as coat color and heavy coat. Oftentimes one characteristic is desired and the other is not, as in the case of a long neck linked to a longer body. It is easy to see why the faddist-type breeders can leave behind them a heritage which in the long run may prove debilitating to the breed.

"In their desire to obtain a certain trait quickly, they are likely to select a specimen which is outstanding for that trait, but they overlook the other undesirable traits that the specimen may also possess. Constant line breeding or inbreeding to such a specimen can easily set up an undesirable pattern of linkage.

"Now, as I emphasized earlier, you as a judge are an educator. What you put up, people will breed to. If you help perpetuate fads and extremes, that is the way those breeds will evolve. If you keep in mind moderation and balance, there is little danger you will be the Pied Piper leading a breed to danger.

"Accept the fact that there are different types within each breed. Accept them for what they are—variations on a theme—and stay with animals which display good temperament, soundness, movement, and condition.

"Now, I am going to emphasize good ring procedures and how to approach the selection of the best specimens.

"You, I am sure, have heard judging called an art and a science. That is true, but it is also a psychological tour de

59

force. Judges must give the impression that they are there to render fair-minded and impartial decisions. To foster this impression there can be no prolonged discussions with familiar exhibitors or favorite handlers in the ring. A little chitchat maybe, but no more. The gallery has its favorites, and will wonder if that innocuous discussion means showing favoritism.

"You must quickly set up the rules of the ring. These include where you will go over the dogs, and how you will gait them. Explain the gait pattern to each exhibitor—some may not have been paying attention. Speak plainly and loudly enough to be understood. When using gestures, be definitive and be sure you are understood.

"Dress the part. Remember you are an authority on the breeds you are judging, and it helps to play the part. Nothing erodes an exhibitor's confidence in a judge as does a too-casually dressed judge. You need not look as if you are going to the Lodge's Annual Dinner, but be presentable.

"Okay, you're in the ring now. You have checked your book and your steward has gotten your class ready. It may be a good idea to have the exhibitors come into the ring in catalog order so you do not have excessive jockeying for ring position. It also helps to get the classes in the ring a bit faster.

"You have already decided where you will go over your dogs, so have the class line up there. Remember, it is a good idea if you can give your gallery a good view, also.

"An important move: stand back from your entries so you can get a total perspective of the entire class. You will not necessarily be able to use this to make selections, but breed types become more apparent from this vantage point.

"Next on the agenda, you may wish to move in closer and verify what you have seen from a distance, and walk down the line checking heads, toplines, and so on.

"Sizing up your class, you need to decide if it is large enough to divide up for gaiting. I use ten as a rule of thumb. Anything over that and I divide the class. To truly see and compare gait, you should move your class around

the ring twice. Be sure to tell this to the exhibitors and tell them where to stop. If you do this there will not be those pileups when the lead exhibitor stops and everyone else slams into him.

"As your dogs go around, you can begin to sort out the quality dogs. These are the dogs with their heads up and their tails going, enjoying the scene. This is the time to appraise quickly the toplines, reach, and drive. Once a class of good dogs is lined up for inspection, they look alike when you survey them from a distance.

"Once you start down the row of prospects, whether you are judging them on the table or on the ground, you should be assessing fine points—head, bite, shoulder placement. You should be looking at the total dog so that those parts remain in balance. A great head has little value on a cow-hocked dog. You should not give 'brownie points' to each part of the dog. How the parts fit together is more important.

"As an exhibitor, you should appreciate, from a judge's eye view, observing how the handlers stack their dogs. As you know, almost every possible angle is employed by exhibitors. A dog that you have just carefully watched go around with its rear high above its withers is suddenly stacked as if it has the best sloping topline you have ever seen. Another dog is 'cranked up' so that its rear is stretched so far you would swear the dog is supporting its weight by its stifles instead of its hind legs. After going over each dog in its artificial stance, you should move each one individually. If you apply what you know about anatomy, you may see a sharp distinction between what is supposed to be and what is.

"As you train your eye, you should be able to evaluate a dog in motion properly. A dog moves as it is built. That you can't fake. A good handler can't help disguising his dog's faults—that's his job. But it is your job to get the best view of the dog possible, so as to evaluate it properly.

"To do this, you need to see the dog moving to and from you to detect proper single tracking, with a straight column of bones. A side view is imperative in order to see reach and foot timing, and to watch for bobbing withers caused by straight shoulders. You can also see topline and sagging or roached backs with this view. The best pattern seems to be a triangle with a long leg, which should be the one where you observe the side view.

"As the dog comes back to you, stop it just as it comes up. Ask the handler to leave it standing naturally. This is a good time to verify that what you felt front and rear in the stacked pose is for real. If you like the dog, send it around in a complete circle so you can assure yourself that indeed this is one of the good ones.

"After gaiting each dog, you might, especially in a large class, put your dogs into a 'good guy' group and an 'also ran' group. After all the dogs have been evaluated, you might look over your 'also ran' group to ensure that you did not overlook a good one. Then excuse them. Many handlers would prefer to leave the ring if they don't have a serious shot at placing. This gives them more time to prepare other dogs or get to the next ring. When you dismiss this group, do it with courtesy and tact. No one *likes* to be excused.

"Turning your attention to the 'good guy' group, it is a good idea to bring them to the center of the ring so the spectators can have a good view of the finalists. You should have made sure that you had more than four dogs left in this group. If you did not, and one of the dogs turned up lame or acted up, you would not have enough dogs to make up your complement of winners.

"In appraising the best specimens it's best once again to get far enough away to get a good perspective of them as a group. If it is a large group, and especially if it is a Specialty show, you might wish to select from the large 'good guy' group the best six or seven specimens, gait the others to ensure you have not left a good one out, and then excuse them. This indicates to this group that they were in until the second cut. It does wonders for their morale.

"Now you are left with the cream of the class. If you are still not sure which ones are to be selected, you might have them face a different direction to get another slant on how they look. Now you must choose. Quickly make your placements by indicating with your fingers your selections. You can do this while the dogs are posed or on the fly. It's your choice, but do it decisively.

"There are a number of common tricks of the trade employed by exhibitors. As a judge you should be aware of them and also be aware of the impact that well-known handlers or important breeders in a certain breed may have on your decision-making process.

"First is the hypnotic stare. This is when an individual stacks his dog, then seeks the judge with his eyes as if to convince him by a level, fixed stare that the judge has to

put the dog up. A variation of this approach is the exhibitor who looks at the judge with pleading eyes—the 'he just has to win' look.

"Then there is the exhibitor who somehow or other lets you know that his dog needs only the points or Best of Winners to finish. This has been a clever ruse used for years, especially with inexperienced judges. After all, the dog must be pretty good if it only needs today's points to finish. At least that's the idea they want to put in your head. It's a sucker play—don't fall for it. Instead give such an exhibitor an icy stare for even daring to think you could be influenced.

"Next is the oblivious groomer. On occasion, as you await the next class, an individual will get into the ring early (but not if you do the catalog order) and stack his dog near where you are seated. He will act as if he is oblivious to you as you sit there. He fluffs the dog's coat, runs a practiced hand over those just beautiful shoulders, then looks up with a blissful look that says his dog is the living end. Remember, no Oscars or Emmys are given at dog shows, so this exhibitor may not get his just reward.

"Another time-worn gimmick is addressing the dog by its registered name as the dog is called upon to gait. The intent is to make sure that you recognize the well-advertised entry. Another Oscar applicant.

"An important point to keep in mind while judging is that looking at a dog without allowing its physical make-up to permeate your mind is futile.

"And, as a prospective judge, you need to develop the ability to give effective reasons for your decisions, both to yourself and to exhibitors. I'll give you some pointers that may help.

"First, since judging is an art based on observations, it is impossible to appraise animals in terms of exact percentages. Different parts of an animal do not have the same value, but since each part is interrelated with, and dependent on, other parts, in the last analysis the animal must be considered as a whole, rather than as a large number of separate parts.

"Second, however, you should learn the points of an animal, and you should master the relative importance of various parts on the basis of anatomy. But to assign a definite percentage value to each part of an animal often leads to confusion. Judging is not based upon a mathematical formula or a compilation of percentages. Instead, it is an analysis which takes solid judgment and a lot of practice.

"Third, to be logical in your analysis, you must cast aside all prejudiced ideas and approach the task in an honest and open-minded manner. In judging, it is important to have unbiased information on what constitutes merit. This means that you should develop early in your judging studies, a spirit of fairness without prejudice.

"You should be careful, however, that your enthusiasm for perfection in certain points does not interfere with your judgment of their total value. For example: One, develop an open mind and be guided by the facts you have at hand. Two, when you allow prejudice or biased opinions to place a class, you are catering to your emotions and basically are disqualifying yourself as a competent judge. Three, observe the animals accurately, weigh the facts in a balanced manner, and conclude with a logical placing, and your 'busts' will be kept to a minimum. Never follow hunches. Judging consists of applied, sound reasoning.

"Be independent, make your own decisions—don't let others decide for you. Pay no attention to ringside applause or comments. However, you should develop your mind along the lines of selection under the guidance of more senior judges in the field. You should always be open-minded to *just* criticism and make your mistakes stepping stones to right thinking instead of stumbling blocks to progress. And you should trust your judgments in the ring over those of the ringside observer, so be honest with yourself and rely on your own independent placing.

"Only in proportion to the extent that you exercise independence of thought will you be able to improve your judging ability. Strengthen your own ability for selecting animals correctly through independent thought, proper guidance, and researched facts.

"A judge often meets trying problems in the ring. These come when large groups of uniformly high-class animals are judged and the decisions are extremely close. Close decisions, regardless of the number of individuals involved, call for considerable emotional stability on the part of the judge. The most useful assistance the judge can possibly have on such occasions lies in his ability to recognize values, in his deep regard for honesty, and in his discipline in independent thought and action. He cannot have confidence in his effort to make decisions unless he has well in hand the basic facts involved. Conscientious judges have only one person to please in making decisions—namely, themselves.

"It is important that you understand that no two individuals will ever see a dog from the same viewpoint. Behavior, style, and gait will seem different to different judges because of their varied backgrounds and their individual breeds. Certainly the Chow breeder and the Sheltie breeder have been emphasizing different features. Matters of judgment are open to differences of opinion too, and if judges at successive shows don't agree, it doesn't mean that either one is blind or dishonest. Let's face it, you can give out only one set of points in each sex, and one Best of Breed. There have to be more losers than winners. Therefore, prepare yourself—there are bound to be more people at each show who may consider you inept than people who think you are the 'greatest.' Don't despair, that's the nature of the game. If you have judged objectively, and handled your ring decisively, put up what *you* think are the best dogs, and walk out of that ring proudly. You have done your best.

"After years of show-going, most of us recognize that judging dogs is far from an exact science. Symmetry, balance, pleasing contours, profile, gait, and expression are artistic terms, and to use them properly one has to have developed an 'eye for a dog.' You need to be aware of the bite, the way the flews hang, the shape and color of the eyes, and all of the little differences that are there if you look hard enough for them, but, of which, few people other than judges are really aware.

"Although a judge must take sufficient time in going over the dogs to note important details, the quality of the judging does not necessarily depend upon the length of time devoted to it. One of the pet peeves of exhibitors and dog show superintendents alike is the judge who does everything but change the oil on a dog while he debates with himself before making a decision. Remember, you are expected to be able to judge between twenty and twenty-five dogs an hour.

"If you learn your breeds well, there are sufficient differences apparent among most dogs to allow you to make up your mind almost as soon as you've seen them. At least to sort out the good ones. While the final confirmation of your first impression requires further examination for less noticeable characteristics, you should develop the capability of making early judgments which will be confirmed by more detailed inspection. It is only occasionally that dogs are so evenly matched that they present any great problems for a good judge, and you may rest assured that the differences are there, even if it takes a little more searching to find them.

"Last, but not least, be a gentleman in the ring at all times. Handle yourself graciously. Whenever possible thank the exhibitors for showing under you. Place your dogs in the ring so that the gallery gets a good view of the activities. And, yes, most of all, express your appreciation to your stewards. Theirs is a tough, often thankless job. Without them your ring wouldn't run as smoothly as it does."

As I flew home, I knew I had received good advice along with an excellent cognac. All that remained was the task of filling out the voluminous forms required by the AKC, visits to at least three breeders of each breed I wanted to judge, and an interview with an AKC field representative.

That was all?

These Denlinger books available in local stores, or write the publisher.

YOUR DOG BOOK SERIES

Illustrated with photographs and line drawings, including chapters on selecting a puppy, famous kennels and dogs, breed history and development, personality and character, training, feeding, grooming, kenneling, breeding, whelping, etc. 5½ x 8½.

YOUR AFGHAN HOUND
YOUR AIREDALE TERRIER
YOUR ALASKAN MALAMUTE
YOUR BASENJI
YOUR BEAGLE
YOUR BORZOI
YOUR BOXER
YOUR BULLDOG
YOUR BULL TERRIER
YOUR CAIRN TERRIER
YOUR CHIHUAHUA
YOUR DACHSHUND
YOUR ENGLISH SPRINGER SPANIEL
YOUR GERMAN SHEPHERD
YOUR GERMAN SHORTHAIRED POINTER
YOUR GREAT DANE

YOUR LHASA APSO
YOUR MALTESE
YOUR MINIATURE PINSCHER
YOUR NORWEGIAN ELKHOUND
YOUR OLD ENGLISH SHEEPDOG
YOUR PEKINGESE
YOUR POMERANIAN
YOUR POODLE
YOUR PUG
YOUR SAMOYED
YOUR SHIH TZU
YOUR SILKY TERRIER
YOUR ST. BERNARD
YOUR VIZSLA
YOUR WELSH CORGI
YOUR YORKSHIRE TERRIER

OTHER DOG BOOKS

THE BEARDED COLLIE
THE BELGIAN SHEEPDOG
BIRD DOGS AND UPLAND GAME BIRDS
THE BOOK OF DOG GENETICS
THE BOSTON TERRIER
THE BOUVIER DES FLANDRES
BREEDING BETTER COCKER SPANIELS
THE BRITTANY
THE BULLMASTIFF
THE CARDIGAN HANDBOOK
THE CHESAPEAKE BAY RETRIEVER
CHINESE NAMES FOR ORIENTAL DOGS
THE CHINESE SHAR-PEI
THE COMPLETE GERMAN SHORTHAIRED POINTER
DOG OBEDIENCE TRAINING MANUAL, VOL. 1
DOG OBEDIENCE TRAINING MANUAL, VOL. 2
DOG OBEDIENCE TRAINING MANUAL, VOL. 3
DOGS IN SHAKESPEARE
DOGS ON THE FRONTIER
DOG TRAINING IS KID STUFF
DOG TRAINING IS KID STUFF COLORING BOOK
THE DYNAMICS OF CANINE GAIT
GAELIC NAMES FOR CELTIC DOGS
GERMAN NAMES FOR GERMAN DOGS
THE GOLDEN RETRIEVER
THE GREAT AMERICAN DOG SHOW GAME

GREAT DANES IN CANADA
GROOMING AND SHOWING TOY DOGS
GUIDE TO JUNIOR SHOWMANSHIP
HOW TO SPEAK DOG
HOW TO TRAIN DOGS FOR POLICE WORK
THE IRISH TERRIER
THE KERRY BLUE TERRIER
THE LABRADOR RETRIEVER
LEADER DOGS FOR THE BLIND
THE MASTIFF
MEISEN BREEDING MANUAL
MEISEN POODLE MANUAL
MR. LUCKY'S TRICK DOG TRAINING
THE NEWFOUNDLAND
THE PHARAOH HOUND
THE PORTABLE PET
RAPPID OBEDIENCE & WATCHDOG TRAINING
RUSSIAN NAMES FOR RUSSIAN DOGS
SHOW DOGS—PREPARATION AND PRESENTATION OF
SKITCH (The Message of the Roses)
THE STANDARD BOOK OF DOG BREEDING
THE STANDARD BOOK OF DOG GROOMING
THE STANDARD BOOK OF KENNEL MANAGEMENT
TOP PRODUCERS—SIBERIAN HUSKYS
THE UNCOMMON DOG BREEDS
YOU AND YOUR IRISH WOLFHOUND

To order any of these books, write to Denlinger's Publishers, P.O. Box 76, Fairfax, VA 22030

For information call (703) 631-1500   VISA and Master Charge orders accepted.

New titles are constantly in production, so please call us to inquire about breed books not listed here.